08225801 · 842025

780.92 MAX
GRIFFITHS
842025

KT-446-238

B.C.H.E. – LIBRARY

00105277

The Contemporary Composers

PETER MAXWELL DAVIES

FOR SIR WILLIAM GLOCK

The Contemporary Composers

Series Editor: Nicholas Snowman

PETER MAXWELL DAVIES

Paul Griffiths

 Robson Books

Acknowledgements
The musical examples, which are printed at sounding pitch,
are reproduced by kind permission of Schott & Co. Ltd.
(Examples 1 and 3–6), Boosey & Hawkes Music Publishers
Ltd. (Examples 7–10), and Novello & Co. Ltd. (Example 2).
Davies's article on his First Symphony appeared originally in
Tempo.

BATH COLLEGE
OF
HIGHER EDUCATION
NEWTON PARK
LIBRARY

CLASS
No. 780.92 MAX G

ACC
No. 842025

FIRST PUBLISHED IN GREAT BRITAIN IN 1982
BY ROBSON BOOKS LTD., BOLSOVER HOUSE, 5–6
CLIPSTONE STREET, LONDON W1P 7EB © 1981 PAUL
GRIFFITHS (EXCEPT PART III). COPYRIGHT © 1961,
1963, 1967, 1969, 1972, 1973, 1977, 1978, 1979, 1980, 1981;
COPYRIGHT © 1981 THIS EDITION PETER MAXWELL
DAVIES (PART III).

British Library Cataloguing in Publication Data

Griffiths, Paul
    Peter Maxwell Davies.—(Contemporary composers; 2)
    I. Title   II. Series
    780'.92'4   ML410.D

    ISBN 0-86051-138-3

All rights reserved. No part of this publication may be
reproduced, stored in a retrieval system, or transmitted in
any form or by any means, electronic, mechanical,
photocopying, recording or otherwise, without prior permission in writing of the publishers.

Printed in Hungary

CONTENTS

EDITOR'S PREFACE

It is no secret that our epoch favours a museological rather than a prospective approach to musical activity. Such a situation is, of course, the reflection of a cultural climate, but it is also the result of problems particular to the evolution of musical language during this century.

Whatever the fundamental causes, the effects are clear. The repertoire of 'classical' music has been extended backwards in time and enlarged with the inclusion of many important works as well as a great number of lesser ones. At the same time the 'standard' works of the eighteenth and nineteenth centuries have become more than ever entrenched in a musical world very largely conditioned by market considerations and thus inimical to contemporary endeavour. One cannot blame record company employees, concert promoters and artists' agents for being more interested in quick turnover than in the culture of their time. The results are inevitable: re-recordings of the same symphonies and operas multiply; performances of the same 'early' music, claiming to be less inauthentic than their rivals, abound; and conductors' careers are made with an ever-diminishing bunch of scores.

Where does this leave the music written yesterday and today? The answer is not encouraging. As far as western Europe and the United States are concerned, contemporary works inhabit a number of well defined ghettos.

In West Germany it is the radio stations that commission

and perform new scores and, naturally enough, their concern is to satisfy their specialist listeners rather than to cultivate a wider public. Except for a certain number of important but brief 'shop window' festivals, contemporary music is hardly a living affair.

In the United States composers find sanctuary in the universities—comfort and security but little contact with the general musical public outside the walls. And in times of economic regression, enterprising and excellent modern music ensembles encounter increasing financial difficulties, whilst symphony orchestras, reliant for their existence on the whims of the rich and generally conservative, play safer than ever.

In the UK, outside the BBC and one or two imaginative enterprises like Glasgow's Musica Nova, the situation is depressing—on the one hand, inadequate state funds spread too thinly, on the other, excellent but hungry orchestras competing for the same marketable fodder. Britain, in spite of at least two recent determined attempts, cannot even boast a modest but representative contemporary music festival worthy of international attention.

France, with its rigorous but narrow education system giving little place to the non-literary arts, has suddenly in these last few years woken up to the charms of music and begun to invest more and more heavily in this new passion. Though it will take years before this musically rootless country can boast the proliferation of performing talent of its neighbours, native respect for the 'intellect' ensures that the music of today is discussed, played and subsidized relatively correctly. Yet in spite of all the activity, contemporary music outside Paris attracts small audiences; the work of 'decentralization' so dear to Gallic politicians is more arduous here than in other countries.

This is not the place for a thorough survey of the status of contemporary music in the world in general. However, it seems clear that even a brief glance at a few different countries reveals the existence of an uneasy relationship between the contemporary public and its music. Certainly, a few independently minded and cultivated musicians seek by their artistic policies to persuade the musical public to accept the endeavours of the present as well as the rich and varied musical traditions and structures of the past.

This new series of books, each introducing a different living composer, seeks to supplement the work of the pathfinders. The scope of the series does not reflect any particular musical 'party line' or aesthetic; its aims are to be representative of what exists, and to supply the listener who stumbles across a new piece at a Prom or on record with the essential facts about its composer—his life, background and work.

London, June 1981   NICHOLAS SNOWMAN

INTRODUCTION

Since this book is intended in the first place for those coming fairly fresh to the music of Peter Maxwell Davies, it may not be out of place to include here a recollection of my own introduction to his work. It was in 1965 that I was taken by a friend at Oxford to a string quartet recital in Magdalen College. The programme consisted of something by Haydn and Schubert's 'Death and the Maiden', with in between the String Quartet from 1961 of Peter Maxwell Davies. The name was unknown to me, for at that time I had heard nothing more extraordinary than Britten's *War Requiem*, but I was comforted by a note in the programme to the effect that the work had been influenced by the Monteverdi Vespers, which, along with thousands of others at that time, I had come to enjoy greatly. The piece itself quickly countered my expectations of familiarity. However, I was sufficiently stirred to seek out that name in each succeeding copy of the *Radio Times*, and through the agency of the BBC I grew to know not only more of Davies's music but also a good deal of contemporary music of all sorts. The dedication of this book is some acknowledgement of that debt.

Others have assisted me at a later stage in this project, and I must thank first the composer himself for his generosity in allowing me to re-publish the notes on his works which make up the third part of the book, and in putting himself at my disposal for the interview sessions which produced the second part. I am also very grateful to Judy Arnold, who arranged those sessions and helped in other ways with her fund of enthusiasm and information. My task was further lightened by Davies's publishers, in particular Sally Cavender at Boosey & Hawkes, David Stevens at Schott and Margaret Perry at Chester Music, all of whom provided me with scores and documentary material. Timothy Day and other members of the staff of the British Institute of Recorded Sound made it possible for me to hear virtually everything Davies has written, and Paul Driver, who is engaged on his own study of the composer, generously drew various articles to my attention. I also owe much to my newspaper, *The Times*, for making it possible for me to visit Orkney on two occasions to cover the St. Magnus Festival and, incidentally, to make the trek across Hoy to the composer's cliff-top dwelling. In matters of classical scholarship I drew shamefacedly on the erudition of Tim Reader.

Davies's rate of production makes it difficult to keep up with his development and to present it within a manageable space: in terms of playing duration his output already rivals that of Schoenberg or Stravinsky. I have thought it best to move quite swiftly and chronologically through his creative career, in four 'movements', separated by interludes which look a little more closely at three important chamber works: the String Quartet (1961), *Antechrist* (1967) and *Ave Maris Stella* (1975). Those who dislike technical analysis may skip the interludes; those who dislike anything else may skip the rest. And those eager to hear the composer's own view will march straight to Parts II and III.

July 1981   P.G.

PROLOGUE: THE MAN

In an age which seems to have lost confidence in its ability to create art—and, in particular, in its ability to create music—it is rare to find a composer who dares to go on tackling the deepest issues of what it is to be human, who dares to create works as meaningfully complex and expressively replete as those of the great nineteenth-century symphonists, who dares to continue producing masterpieces. Peter Maxwell Davies is such a composer. Although creative abundance has never been alone a mark of quality, and is perhaps least so in our own century, the rate of Davies's output is indeed a measure of the pressure of his ideas and his need to get them out. This urge to communicate has led him increasingly to develop and refine a language which is unmistakably his own, unmistakably of the second half of the twentieth century, and yet which holds to a traditional belief in music as continuous thought, conveyed in sound and guided by the powers of harmony. And this belief, wholly opposed to a notion of art as decoration or entertainment, makes Davies's a music of extraordinary humanity—a challenge to the listener that through it he should understand himself—even when it is dealing, because it has to, with the darkest corners of the mind. Davies has never fought shy of concerning himself with extreme emotional states and black negation, but the act of encompassing such material is one of profound sympathy, an enlargement of the human spirit.

Davies was born on 8 September 1934 in Manchester, and so

between the ages of five and ten he was a schoolboy in a country at war. No doubt this had its effect on him: the story is told how he declared his own little kingdom among the streets, with its own particular customs and language. But he was also preparing himself more peaceably for the business of influencing people's minds. As he says in the second part of this book, a visit to a Gilbert and Sullivan operetta when he was four set him on the road to being a composer, and though this might appear an unlikely first encounter with musical theatre for the later composer of *Eight Songs for a Mad King*, it showed him worlds beyond an industrial city on the edge of war. When he was eight he began to learn the piano and to teach himself to compose, partly from books, partly by devouring any music he could get hold of. By the time he was in his early teens, and a pupil at Leigh Grammar School, he was familiar with the whole standard repertory of piano, chamber and orchestral music, and this firm grounding in the central tradition, above all in the music of Beethoven, has been always of the utmost importance to his own creative work. Most especially, the basic principles of sonata form—those of presenting musical themes, developing them and bringing them to some kind of resolution—run through the whole of his output, beginning with his opus 1, the Trumpet Sonata of 1955.

That work, which had been preceded by a vast quantity of juvenilia (some of which Davies retains in his possession), was written while its composer was a student at Manchester University, where he read music, and at the Royal Manchester College of Music (now the Royal Northern College). His years as a student in Manchester, from 1952 to 1957, expanded his musical awareness both forwards and backwards in time. Stimulated partly by a desire to seek out parts of the repertory that were not being taught, he began to learn a great deal from medieval and renaissance music, particularly from the ways plainsong melodies were used by composers of the fifteenth and sixteenth centuries to create works of great formal elaboration and contrapuntal artifice. This, too, has remained extremely important to his musical thinking, and it is worth noting that his interest in what has come to be known as 'early music' dates from some years before the revival of a public appetite for such music encouraged by such musicians as David Munrow in England and Noah Greenberg in the United States. At the time he must have felt himself very much alone in interesting himself in such names as those of Machaut, Dufay, Josquin—and Taverner, already chosen during this period as the subject of a future opera.

He was less by himself in his concern with new music, for he found in Manchester a small circle of fellow students who shared his enthusiasm for the work of Stravinsky, Schoenberg, Berg and Webern, and for the music then being written in Europe. Very little of this was then available in print: Stockhausen's *Kontra-Punkte* and his first book of piano pieces, Boulez's Flute Sonatina and his first two piano sonatas, a few works by Nono and that was about all. But here was the music that excited Davies and his colleagues, a highly talented group including the composers Harrison Birtwistle and Alexander Goehr, the pianist John Ogdon and the trumpeter-conductor Elgar Howarth. And it was within the context of this new European music—within the context, too, of Beethovenian argument and an emerging grasp of medieval and renaissance techniques—that Davies produced his first acknowledged compositions, the Trumpet Sonata written for Howarth and the Five Piano Pieces (1955–6) written for Ogdon.

Such works were not calculated to go down well at the time in England, where 'new music' meant the later symphonies of Vaughan Williams or the operas of Britten, not *Le Marteau sans Maître* or *Zeitmasse*. Davies reacted against the conservatism and insularity of British music in his first published article, appearing in the March 1956 number of *The Score*, where he made a combative defence of the obligation upon a composer to gain technical competence through the study of the works of others—and here he included the 'more ancient' composers, suggesting already his interest in the possibilities revealed by early music. What emerges most strongly, however, is his insistence on analysis, then very much undervalued in British musical education, and on compositional technique. Only through the stringent application of technique, he has said, can a composer be certain that his music is definitely his own and not an imitation of somebody else's. And his compositions of this period reveal how much expertise he had gained from his studies of early, classical and contemporary composers, as well as from music culturally more distant. There was a group of pieces based on Indian music, though of these he saved only *Stedman Doubles* for clarinet and percussion (1955, see note, p. 135).

In 1957 Davies went from Manchester to Rome, with an Italian government scholarship to continue his compositional training under Goffredo Petrassi, and he remained in Italy for eighteen months, during which time he began to establish a reputation as a composer of extremely intricate, tightly organized music. His wind sextet, *Alma Redemptoris Mater*, was played at the 1958 festival of the International Society for Contemporary Music in Strasbourg, and his first orchestral work, *Prolation*, followed at the 1959 festival in Rome, while in the same year his sonata, *St. Michael*, for two choirs of wind instruments had its first performance at the Cheltenham Festival. At such a venue, and indeed in England generally at this time, Davies could only be regarded as an *enfant terrible*, but it was to England that he returned in 1959.

He was still, of course, far from able to make a living as a composer, and so he took a post as music master at Cirencester Grammar School. But though, according to his own account, he entered teaching simply as a painless way of making money, his Cirencester appointment was to bring about a quite new approach to school music and, for the composer himself, a daily practical contact with music-making that was to leave him greatly more confident in his technique. He was obliged to write pieces that could be guaranteed to work, stretching his young performers but not confusing them or presenting them with material that they could not possibly understand. The fearsome complexity of his first published compositions was obviously not going to be suitable for children to perform or to comprehend, and so he had to develop a simpler manner. He had also to overcome any inhibitions he may have had about making his art dramatic and expressive.

16

All this he did with astonishing success in a very short time. By 1962, when he left Cirencester, he had created at least one work, the carol sequence *O Magnum Mysterium*, which has remained a classic of the school repertory, apart from writing other carols and orchestral pieces for children to play. He had also made a name for himself as a proponent of new educational methods. No longer were children to spend their music periods singing third-rate folk-song settings or being instructed in 'musical appreciation': the emphasis was on the creative practice of music. Davies encouraged his pupils to compose and to improvise, working in small groups and discovering things for themselves, while he would be on hand to introduce techniques of composition, analysis and performance when they were needed.

On leaving Cirencester he took up a Harkness Fellowship that enabled him to pursue further studies at Princeton University under Roger Sessions and Earl Kim. He has acknowledged a debt to both of these teachers, notably by dedicating to them respectively *A Mirror of Whitening Light* (1976–7) and the Seven In Nomine (1963–4), but it is not easy to see what the composer of *O Magnum Mysterium* or the String Quartet (1961) still had to learn that he could not gain from himself. The real importance of his two years at Princeton was that he was enabled to think and compose as much as he wanted, and the result was that he was able to begin serious work on the opera *Taverner*, dealing with events in the life of the Tudor composer John Taverner, a work which he had been planning since 1956.

In fact, Davies had prepared himself musically for the opera before he went to Princeton, composing the First Fantasia on an In Nomine of John Taverner for the 1962 Proms: a Second Fantasia, written in Princeton after the first act of the opera had been completed, was commissioned by the London Philharmonic Orchestra and played by them in the Royal Festival Hall, London, on 30 April 1965. There were also commissions during this period of increasing activity and acceptance from the English Chamber Orchestra (Sinfonia, 1962), the BBC (*Shakespeare Music*, 1964), the Melos Ensemble (Seven In

17

Nomine) and the UNESCO Conference on Music in Education (*The Shepherd's Calendar*, 1965)

Thus, by the time he returned from Princeton to England, in 1964, Davies was coming to be regarded as one of the leaders of a new generation of British composers, and so too were his Manchester colleagues, Goehr and Birtwistle. The three of them organized the Wardour Castle Summer School of Music in 1964 and 1965, and though Goehr's closer attachment to the great Viennese tradition was giving his music an increasingly classical feel, Birtwistle's early music shows very clearly a development parallel with that of Davies. Birtwistle even followed the road to Princeton, in 1966, while Davies that year was composer-in-residence at the University of Adelaide.

Then, in 1967, Birtwistle and Davies together formed their own performing ensemble, the Pierrot Players, consisting of the sextet required for Schoenberg's *Pierrot Lunaire*—soprano, flautist, clarinettist, violin/viola player, cellist and pianist—together with a percussionist and with the two composers acting as conductors. The group gave their début concert in the Queen Elizabeth Hall, London, on 30 May 1967, when the programme included Davies's instrumental septet, *Antechrist*, as overture and Birtwistle's music theatre work, *Monodrama*, subsequently withdrawn. It was thus Birtwistle who initiated the Pierrot Players' involvement with music theatre, though before long Davies was moving in that direction himself: indeed, he had already prepared for such a course with *Revelation and Fall* (1966), a highly dramatic setting of a poem by Georg Trakl for soprano and sixteen players. After that, and once he had completed *Taverner*, he was in a position to make the concert hall a theatre of extreme emotion and spiritual questing in *Eight Songs for a Mad King* and *Vesalii Icones*, both presented for the first time at Pierrot Players concerts in 1969.

These works, focusing on a raving, insane monarch and a near-naked dancer as Christ, were greeted on one side by shock and outrage, and on the other with intense excitement. The only certainty was that never again could Davies be neatly categorized as a well-behaved composer of the *avant-garde*: he was very obviously an artist with his own entirely individual vision. So it was inevitable that the co-operation with Birtwistle, who was also now set on his own path after his opera, *Punch and Judy* (1966–7), would become ever more difficult to sustain. In 1970 the Pierrot Players were disbanded and then instantly re-formed as the Fires of London, under Davies's sole direction.

Since that time Davies has continued to produce a stream of compositions for his own group, ranging from music theatre pieces to instrumental solos, from arrangements and distortions of other music (by Purcell, Bach, Wagner and many others) to highly demanding chamber works. Until 1980, when the pressures of creative work caused him to cut down on conducting, he appeared regularly with the Fires, giving concerts in Britain and on tour abroad, and with them he established a composer-performer relationship of rare intimacy. His musical influence on the group was very evident even in their performances of music by other composers, not least in their celebrated version of *Pierrot Lunaire* with Mary Thomas, a blood-curdling soloist, backed by instrumental playing that highlighted what is most chilling and forceful in the score. And though the ensemble performed many new works by younger composers, the 'house style', coming from Davies, gave almost everything they did an imprint of him.

Naturally, given the eminent practicality in writing for particular performers that Davies had developed during his Cirencester days, the influences also worked the other way. Mary Thomas's histrionic skills and her extraordinary vocal virtuosity have contributed to all his works with solo soprano, and most particularly to two theatrical *tours de force: Miss Donnithorne's Maggot* (1974) and *The Medium* (1981). Similarly, the almost savage brilliance and hard edge of Alan Hacker's clarinet playing are written into such pieces as *Hymnos* (1967), and Stephen Pruslin's concentration and musical intelligence have their tribute in the Piano Sonata (1981). Moreover, the simple existence of the Fires has been a continuous encouragement to Davies to write new works for them, and in doing so to find ever new ways of using a grouping that a less imaginative

19

composer might have found limiting. The repertory he has produced for them, comprising nearly fifty original works and arrangements, is sufficient to show that this is not so.

Meanwhile, of course, composing for the Pierrot Players and Fires was far from exhausting Davies's creative energies: on the contrary, it seems to have fuelled them. Before the late Sixties his output was respectable but moderate, whereas since then it has been quite astonishing, with most years seeing a fair handful of major compositions. 1969, for instance, apart from *Eight Songs* and *Vesalii Icones*, witnessed the completion of two orchestral works, *Worldes Blis* and *St. Thomas Wake*, of which the former was received with rude incomprehension when it was first performed at the Proms that year, while the latter, thanks largely to its pastiche foxtrots, soon became one of Davies's most popular and frequently performed works. Both works were conducted at their premières by the composer himself, though the role of orchestral conductor is not one he has often chosen to fulfil

In the year following these two orchestral pieces, 1970, Davies went to the island of Hoy in the Orkneys for the first time and quickly decided he must live there. The search for isolation was typical. Though he is a man of great personal charm, humour, gentleness and courtesy—by no means a misanthrope—he has always found he worked best in seclusion. On his return from Princeton, in 1964, he had moved into a remote cottage in the Dorset countryside; Hoy offered him a still greater degree of inaccessibility. In 1974 he moved there permanently, and settled not just on this most forbidding of the Orkney islands but in its deserted village of Rackwick, far from the main centres of its sparse population, and not just in Rackwick but in a croft that is its far-flung cliff-top outpost.

The influence of Orcadian landscape, legend and literature on Davies's music since 1970 has been profound, as the next section of this book will indicate. But, paradoxically, his Orkney period has been a period also of increasing public recognition in the wider world. In 1970–1 he composed music for two films by Ken Russell, *The Devils* and *The Boy Friend*, and in 1972 *Taverner* had its world première at Covent Garden, on

July 12 (the opera had been finished in 1968, though part of it had to be rewritten in 1970 after a fire in the composer's Dorset cottage). Also in the early Seventies came the first recordings of *Eight Songs for a Mad King* and *Vesalii Icones* to join a discography that until then included only *O Magnum Mysterium* and a scattering of smaller pieces. There was also a steady flow of important commissions, from the BBC for the masque *Blind Man's Buff* (1972) and the chamber opera *The Martyrdom of St. Magnus* (1976), from the Bath Festival for *Ave Maris Stella* (1975) and the Edinburgh Festival for *The Lighthouse* (1979), from Jesus College, Oxford, for *From Stone to Thorn* (1971) and Uppsala University for *Westerlings* (1976–7), from the Scottish National Orchestra for *Stone Litany* (1973) and the London Sinfonietta for *A Mirror of Whitening Light* (1976–7). Davies has also become highly regarded as a teacher, transmitting his creative excitement and thoughtfulness—but not his particular style—to such younger composers as Gillian Whitehead. And in 1980 he became musical director of the Dartington Summer School, where his geniality and his acute mind have been particularly apposite.

But if all this suggests a composer moving into his forties with security and steady achievement, Davies's continuing capacity to astonish was forcibly emphasized in 1976 when the Philharmonia Orchestra announced that the work they had commissioned from him had revealed itself as a symphony. The first performance of the work, under Simon Rattle at the Festival Hall on 2 February 1978, was an occasion comparable only with the first night of *Taverner* for the sense of excitement within the audience, the conviction that something of great moment was being unveiled; and the success of the symphony led not only to the speedy release of a recording but also to a commission from the Boston Symphony Orchestra for a successor. This had its première, conducted by Seiji Ozawa, in Boston on 26 February 1981.

Another, if less surprising, departure of the late Seventies was the establishing of the St. Magnus Festival as an annual Orkney event covering the few days around the midsummer solstice. If Davies was to feel himself part of the working

21

community in the Orkneys, he naturally wanted to show his neighbours what he was up to: he had already, indeed, taken the Fires of London to Kirkwall for occasional concerts before the festival was founded. At the same time, the St. Magnus Festival provides opportunities for Orkney people to hear a great variety of other music, and it has quickly become accepted as a part of the life of the islands, thanks in no small measure to the skill and generosity which Davies has shown in writing pieces for local amateur musicians and children to perform: the Festival has seen the premières of three operatic works for schoolchildren—*The Two Fiddlers* (1978), *Cinderella* (1980) and *The Rainbow* (1981)—as well as of the cantata, *Solstice of Light* (1979), devised for the St. Magnus Singers of Kirkwall Cathedral.

In Orkney, then, Davies has found the personal kingdom he had been looking for since his boyhood in Manchester and found, too, a place where he can be of service to others. Orkney provides him with the opportunities to exercise both functions of the artist: to create and explore his own realms of imagination, and to provide intellectual and emotional recreation for an audience. The reconciliation of these two roles, symbolized in several of his works by the figures of King and Jester, is no easy matter in a time when public taste is much more for the art of the past than that of the present: this is something that Davies, like Schoenberg before him, has had to recognize in his music. However, the new spaciousness and confidence of his symphonies, and of the works which surround them, suggests a composer with the power to create his own worlds and the certainty that an audience will be found to inhabit them.

Part One

An Introduction to the Music

1 LEARNING AND TEACHING

The Sonata for Trumpet and Piano, a short three-movement work of 1955, has a position in Davies's output somewhat similar to that of the Flute Sonatina in Boulez's: it was his 'op. 1'; it is much nearer to classical serial technique than anything that followed; and it announces straight away a new musical personality, one of dynamism, humour and intent concentration. There is even some kinship with the Boulez piece in matters of rhythmic style, texture and serial handling, perhaps because at this stage in their careers both composers were strongly influenced by Messiaen and Schoenberg. However, the exultant and at times downright cheerful Davies work only occasionally shares the frenzy and the instability of the Boulez, and in form its miniature movements are obviously less ambitious than Boulez's sonata synthesis.

They are also much closer to classical patterns. The outer movements can both be seen as little sonata-allegros, and the first movement in particular is anxious to make its harmonic shape clearly felt. It opens with a three-note call which provides one of the movement's basic harmonic elements, often appearing as a perfect fifth lying over a minor third. Yet the motif is not part of the work's series. It may be regarded as an assertion of the composer's right to establish his own rules (the personal signature here was rescued from juvenilia and was later to be enshrined as the first idea in the opera,

Taverner), but it is also there to secure a pervading harmonic consistency against which the serial shapes can be illuminated. Another technique which Davies uses to make clear his harmonic intentions is the simple one of emphasizing a note by insistent repetition. It is also characteristic that the first movement's theme should be followed at once by its nihilistic opposite, the chromatic scale, played in the same rhythm and draining away the theme's personality. The ensuing argument depends largely on antipathies among the three elements that have been introduced—the motif, the series and the scale—and rises to a climax, after which, in what is clearly a recapitulation section, the serial theme softly returns in a retrograde form with doubled rhythmic values.

It has seemed worth considering Davies's first published movement in some detail because it contains so many features which have continued to be important in his music: the search for a harmonic logic which aurally involves the listener in the music's forming, the extrapolation of harmonic characteristics from a small cell to a large form, the essentially traditional discourse with its preparations, contrasts and resolutions, the speed of thought and, most distinctive of all, the immediate confrontation of an idea with its subversive negative.

After the Trumpet Sonata came the set of Five Pieces for Piano (1955–6), whose title alludes to the important example of Schoenberg while also suggesting that these are independent items, which they are not: the set is really a work in five movements. The exercises in strict counterpoint that had been carried out in the Trumpet Sonata have borne fruit, and the piano is now used almost throughout as an instrument for the weaving of complex polyphony in three or four parts, showing some indebtedness to Schoenberg but even more to the sonatas of Boulez. Schoenberg is again recalled by the 'Hauptstimme' indications and the stress marks used to show the musical prosody, though the importance attached to durational quantities and rhythmic cells is an inheritance from Messiaen and Indian music. However, despite all these various influences working on the music, the Five Pieces have a quite individual tone of intense and active contemplation, arising in part from oscillations among the pitches of a small group, as if ideas are constantly being weighed and considered from different angles.

In his next composition Davies frankly acknowledged for the first time the example provided by his medieval forebears, for *Alma Redemptoris Mater* (1957) is a wind sextet based on the plainsong Marian antiphon and also on the setting by Dunstable, itself an elaboration of the chant. The complete works of Dunstable had been published in the Musica Britannica series in celebration of the quincentenary of Dunstable's death (1953), but perhaps Davies's attention was drawn to this particular work by its quotation in full in Gustave Reese's standard textbook, *Music in the Middle Ages*. At the same time he was following a tradition in English music from Dunstable to Taverner in choosing a Marian subject for a polyphonic treatment which is both public ceremonial and personal contemplation.

Dunstable provided the work with certain formal principles. His antiphon is in three sections, triple counterpoint enclosing a central duo, and Davies's piece is similarly in three movements, two andantes around a presto. Just as Dunstable's duo is made up of phrases of nine, eight and ten dotted minims (in modern notation), so Davies's presto follows a pattern of even contraction and expansion in having sections of fifteen, twelve and eighteen 2/4 bars (the duple measure is used throughout the piece, as in much of the piano set, making rhythmic designs quite clear). Moreover, the similarities between the first and last phrases of the Dunstable duo are mirrored in the Davies presto. The first section has a cantus firmus, or underlying melody, split into three fragments, with light-footed counterpoint around, and in the third section the cantus substructure is shifted bodily to the end, where it appears unadorned, with the counterpoint now preceding it though altered in many respects. The actual musical material is developed largely from the rising six-note figure, C—E—F—G—A—C, with which the *Alma Redemptoris Mater* plainsong begins, and though Davies works this hard, he recaptures on his own terms the chant's graceful, ornate unfolding.

Applying quasi-serial procedures to plainsong fragments, as in *Alma Redemptoris Mater*, was to remain one of Davies's most characteristic and powerful technical tools. He used it again immediately, looking this time to chants from the Requiem Mass, in *St. Michael* (1957), another work for wind instruments, but replacing the closely woven chamber ensemble with the extrovert formation of orchestral wind in two choirs, one of double woodwind plus horn, the other a brass octet. The instrumentation is close to that of Stravinsky's Symphonies of Wind Instruments, and the manner is similarly austere, almost liturgical. However, the precedent to which Davies appeals most directly is older: the groupings are obviously modelled on those of Gabrieli's canzonas and sonatas, and there is the same delight in antiphonal display, especially in the last of the five movements, where bold chords are heaved from one ensemble to another. Beyond that, the work looks again to medieval and early renaissance polyphony. As in *Alma Redemptoris Mater*, the texture is often a fine-spun web of overlapping motifs, but there are also canonic structures which rise more or less clearly to the surface at different times, as well as forms founded on isorhythmic girders.

In harmonic style *St. Michael* differs from the sextet, its urgent dynamism driving right through the five contrasted movements. The first of these is a moderato introduction, followed by a vigorous allegro built like the first movement of *Alma Redemptoris Mater* on a cantus firmus repeated in sections of unequal length. The middle movement is very slow, pondering motifs of two or three notes in richly stressful harmony, and then a quick movement for woodwinds alone leads into the tremendous final acceleration from adagio to vivace, where the trumpet returns from the sonata with jagged signals to impel the music to its hectic climax.

At first Davies assembled these movements under the straight-forward title 'Sonata': only after the first performance was the work renamed in honour of the saint on one of whose feast days its composition was begun. Possibly Davies wanted to give his work the same dedication as that of one of Taverner's great festal masses, *O Micael*, for he was already giving thought to an opera on the life of that composer, but the archangel is also an entirely fitting patron for a work in which plainsong elements are tested in the fire of musical imagination. For though on one level plainsong is simply a reservoir of useful musical material, and though its use in making instrumental music has a tradition in England going back to the sixteenth-century *Mulliner Book* and beyond, Davies has always worked with the view that the statement of a chant melody carries with it implicitly the statement of its text, and so to edit and distort such a melody must be to explore religious truth. Another two years were to pass before he was to set a sacred text, but *St. Michael* is already an instrument of spiritual investigation.

The work was written almost literally under the shadow of St. Michael, or at least of his statue surmounting the Castell Sant' Angelo, for Davies had now moved to Rome for further study under Petrassi. There he also wrote his first work for full orchestra, *Prolation* (1957–8), a twenty-minute movement which in formal complexity marks a considerable advance on anything he had composed hitherto, and which is also a quite extraordinary feat of rhythmic engineering. In medieval music 'prolation' was the term for the relationship of semibreve to minim: 'major prolation' indicated values of 3:1 and 'minor prolation' values of 2:1. Extrapolating from this, Davies creates a work in which the sequence of ratios 10:4:7:6:5 governs relative durations at every level from that of tiny details to that of whole sections, and the development of the rhythmic grouping is coupled with the metamorphosis of a five-note pitch formula.

In its complex facture the work obviously relates to the more speculative enterprises of his continental colleagues, and the orchestral writing shows how much Davies had been impressed by Nono's highly divided yet dynamized textures. However, the strength and range of the harmonic forces generated by the formula leave little doubt as to the identity of the composer.

After the third major section, Vigoroso, the texture thins, often to a single line, and the music begins a long process of condensation around the formula as gradually it is built up in woodwind chords in the introductory bars of each new subsection. The tempo accelerates but the sense of meditation on a fixed object grows ever more intense.

Other, smaller matters are equally personal. There are no unpitched percussion instruments except for a set of five suspended cymbals, change rung to punctuate the rhythmic argument in its later stages, and the tuned percussion has a fair share of the musical interest: especially prominent is the xylophone, which sounds a curiously hollow, ironic note over the tortuous orchestral workings. Another characteristic feature is the use of trumpets as signallers and the investment of emotional weight in the strings, even though the marking 'Lento con grand'espressione' is not fully justified by the nature of the material, as soon such instructions would be. Above all, the work demonstrates Davies's ability to create large stretches of music which have a real feeling of tempo, not just a metronomic value applied fairly indiscriminately, and this is established firmly by the instrumentation, the use of particular gestures (most obviously the pressing single-note crescendos of the opening vivace, looking forward as far as the first movement of the First Symphony) and, most importantly, the different speeds of harmonic movement, thrusting at the start, contemplative in the lento, coming always to rest in the final sections.

Prolation shows Davies heeding the advice he was to give to young composers in his 1959 article in *The Listener*, insisting that 'we must study Continental thought, understand it, absorb its principles, criticize constructively, and, in the light of the experience of the music of the past, take the next step forward'. And without naming the work, he seems to be thinking of this first orchestral piece in the same article when he goes on to give his view that 'rhythmic and dynamic serialism, applied to short note-rows, can be used to build up large musical structures whose relationships are clear to the ear'. While as far as pitch organization is concerned, he concludes: 'If one's material is properly organized, no incongruous tonal hierarchy will suggest itself insidiously, and the judicious use of a few notes transposed into contrasting regions provides interest and even drama.' One may argue about the possibility of eradicating tonal hearing, but with reference to *Prolation* the second part of this statement remains irrefutable.

There came next various smaller works, including in the Sextet (1958) a remarkable premonition of the ensemble with which Davies would later associate himself, for the piece is scored for the Fires of London team of flute, clarinet, violin, cello, piano and percussion (in 1972 it was revised as a septet with the addition of a guitar). There was also music to be written for the children of Cirencester Grammar School, including the set of *Five Klee Pictures* for orchestra (1960), where the original paintings inspire musical images of great verve and precision. They are images strong enough to appeal immediately to children, like the block-chord march which is brutally and mechanically snapped up by unpitched percussion in 'A Crusader', and simple enough to be quickly explained in terms of compositional technique. Yet, despite the vast difference of scale from *Prolation*, they are wholly characteristic of Davies, and they even contain discoveries to be taken up in adult works. Most remarkable in this respect is the fourth piece, 'Stained-Glass Saint', a miniature Mahlerian adagio which at its climax is grotesquely mocked by a birdcall effect, as if the praying saint had turned to show a demon's grin.

Nothing so shocking had happened yet in Davies's professional music, which in 1959 included the octet *Ricercar and Doubles on 'To Many a Well'*, and the Five Motets. The chamber piece returns to the methods of *Alma Redemptoris Mater*, using not a plainsong but a medieval English carol, though it is more playful and dance-like, with the ricercar re-presented in two 'doubles' or variations, first as a scherzo and trio, then as a slow movement. The wholesale reinterpretation of a musical argument had occurred before in Davies's music (it is instructive to compare, for instance, the opening of the lento of *Prolation* with the corresponding passage in the earlier vivace), but in *Ricercar and Doubles* it gains an ironic wit that was to become ever sharper in future twists of meaning.

The Five Motets were originally composed for four soloists

and two antiphonally placed choirs, but in 1962 Davies reduced somewhat the music's fearsome difficulty by providing instrumental support, though without altering the wide intervals, the frequent changes of time signature and the Nono-like splintering of lines across different voices. This was his first published vocal work, and in it he put together a sequence of texts that make up a great calling on Christ. The main pillars of this monumental work, related to what was then recent in Stravinsky's output, are its odd-numbered movements, the first an invocation of Christ in a naming of his multitude of attributes ('Spes, via, vita'), the third a flooding celebration of Him as divine light ('O lux'), the fifth a slow chordal awaiting ('Atollite portas'). In between come movements which are more lightly scored and function as interludes, considering Christ in relation to his mother ('Alma redemptoris mater', not in any obvious way related to the chamber piece) and to the martyr Eulalia ('Nec mora', a duet for soprano and contralto in whole-tone but quite un-Debussyan harmony).

In 1960 Davies followed the motets with a very much simpler work for school resources, *O Magnum Mysterium*, which consists of four unaccompanied carols, two instrumental sonatas and a concluding fantasia for organ (see note, p. 136). Like the *Five Klee Pictures*, the whole work is built from the motif of a semitone plus a whole tone, and again the children's music is skilfully made to meet their practical and intellectual needs. In the carols Davies evolved his own very attractive modality, using a scale (on F in three of the four) with a prominent flattened third and fifth, and block harmony which often opens and closes fanwise, duskily coloured with seconds, sevenths and tritones. This simple style, appropriately reverent yet intimate in feeling, was to serve later for a setting of *The Lord's Prayer* (1962) as well as for more carols, *Ave Maria—Hail Blessed Flower* (1961), *Ave, Plena Gracia* (1964) and sets of four (1961-2) and five (1966), all of these following the precedent of *O Magnum Mysterium* in using medieval texts.

The sonatas of *O Magnum Mysterium* are meditations on the mystery of the incarnation announced in the title carol, and they show Davies's awareness that to consider a musical line is to consider its associated verbal meaning. The first sonata, 'Puer natus', is based on a cantus firmus which paraphrases the treble line of the 'O magnum mysterium' carol: this is stated plain in Webernian timbre-melody, giving the impression that the instruments are giving voice to the theme, and then progressively embellished. There is also a harmonic interlude which provides the seed for the second sonata, 'Lux fulgebit'. Davies here demands modest improvisation, as he had already in the *Klee Pictures* and was to do again in *Te Lucis Ante Terminum* (1961), a successor to *O Magnum Mysterium* with three choral verses separated by two for instruments, these latter standing as a record of how far the Cirencester orchestra had advanced since the earlier work.

As a meditation on the humanity and divinity of Christ, *O Magnum Mysterium* is immediately related to the Five Motets, and the image of divine light is central to both works. However, realizing that ambitious school music has to be performed by children but for adults, Davies decided to end *O Magnum Mysterium* with a vastly more wide-ranging organ solo. The gesture is that of Bach in concluding his D minor violin partita with the massive chaconne, or of Beethoven in finishing his op. 130 quartet with the 'Grosse Fuge', but still more so, for the gulf between the two worlds is so much greater, and dramatically emphasized in performance by the fact that the child musicians are left silent on the platform while the unseen organist puts the adult case.

The fantasia is an argument on the same subject, the same three-note motif, but explores much more complex and diverse harmonic areas. It begins with a long crescendo over an accelerating bass in which the basic motif is repeatedly transposed upwards in ever shorter values. After this preparation the ground shape lends itself to further development in another acceleration of gathering complexity and power, rising to a tumultuous climax which is succeeded, as so often in Davies's music, by a tantalizingly slow withdrawal (this happens also in, for example, the First Taverner Fantasia and, under rather different circumstances, *Ave Maris Stella*).

Since the fantasia is designed to be played after the carols from which it takes its musical material, the connection in terms of subject matter, implicit in such works as *St. Michael*, becomes for the first time unavoidable, and the far harmonic venturing and force of the piece have made it seem to some a sacrilegious comment on what has gone before. But this is surely not Davies's intention. *O Magnum Mysterium* should be seen rather as passing from the simple narration of the carols on to the passive adoration of the sonatas and so to the active meditative effort of the fantasia in trying to comprehend the meaning of Christ's nativity, looking at it from all angles, exploring its implications. Nevertheless, the composer is unlikely not to have realized how nearly strenuous investigation assimilates itself to parody.

Davies's next major effort at Cirencester was a re-creative exercise, a performance of parts of the Monteverdi Vespers, but this was not without creative consequences. Through studying and adapting the music he gained insights into it which led directly on to the composition of the String Quartet (1961), the *Leopardi Fragments* (also 1961) and the Sinfonia for chamber orchestra (1962, see note, p. 138). The second of these, like the motet 'Nec mora', is a duet for soprano and contralto, this time on a larger scale and with octet accompaniment, but the style is more relaxed and sensuous, the whole-tone harmony changed from tritonal austerity to the clear light of thirds and sixths. However, if Monteverdi provided musical suggestions for this development, the expressive cue came from the lines of Leopardi, at once dark and radiant, the first secular text Davies had set and one very much suited to the intense brilliance of his music.

INTERLUDE: STRING QUARTET

Several factors conspire to make Davies's Quartet a suitable
case for more detailed examination at this stage. It is a compact
piece for four instruments and occupying only ten pages of
score, with a playing duration of thirteen minutes. Then again,
although none of Davies's published works could be described
in any way as faltering or juvenile, the Quartet does mark his
attainment of a versatile technique which benefits from the
examples provided by the Austro-German symphonic tradition
as much as by medieval and renaissance music, and which is
utterly distinctive. The work also embodies, often for the first
time, features which will recur in various pieces over the next
few years. In matters of formal principle and harmonic
method, for instance, it is very close to the Second Taverner
Fantasia (1964), though in that work the basic pattern is
reversed and greatly expanded: the Quartet begins with an
adagio that takes up the Mahlerian strain from the *Five Klee
Pictures* (this was a new departure in Davies's professional
music) and then continues with a sequence of fast sections
containing a continuous process, whereas in the orchestral
fantasia the adagio comes after the more forceful development,
though both works end in a totally unexpected throwaway
manner.

Like the Sinfonia, the Quartet begins with a statement of its
fundamental material:

which turns out to be an aural analysis of the main line from the refrain of Davies's own carol *Ave Maria—Hail Blessed Flower:*

A-ve Ma - ri - a,   A - ve Ma - ri - a,   gra-cia De - i   ple - na.

The line is divided in the Quartet version into three phases corresponding to preparation, rise and climax with fast descent. With its outlines thus clarified, its internal construction is elucidated with the aid not only of the instrumentation but also of the rhythmic values: minor seconds have duration ratios of 2:1 (B—C, D—E♭), major seconds ratios of 3:1 (A—G, C—D), minor thirds ratios of 1:1 (A—C, E♭—C, D—B) and major thirds ratios of 3:2 (G—B). These connections of interval and rhythm are maintained with a fair degree of rigour in the adagio, where they usefully draw attention to motivic recurrences, particularly when these concern the even values of minor thirds, and the same relationships are upheld to a more limited extent in the remainder of the work.

Example 1 is the beginning not only of the adagio but also of the cantus firmus which runs right through it, and which is

36

printed in red notes to distinguish it from the decorative
melismas around: the obvious precedent for this was not so
much Boulez's *Constellation*, where entire systems are either red
or green, as the use of notational coloration in medieval music,
where red notes indicated a change of metre. The cantus
repeats the ground idea, with variations, twelve times, the idea
being transposed on to each of its own notes in turn, so that the
whole section follows the harmonic outline of Example 1.
Meanwhile, the black-note embellishments which, unlike the
cantus, allow some rhythmic freedom, add touches of the same
and other harmonic areas:

In this example the cantus is in the first violin and is based
on the ground idea transposed on to C (we are in the fourth
subsection). The first figure in the second violin and that in the
cello emphasize this dominant harmonic area by using the
same mode, while the viola refers to the transposition on to G
and the second violin to that on to D (always these decorations
use transpositions on to notes of the ground idea). At the same
time the example shows continuing interval-rhythm cor-

respondences, notably in the preservation of the 1:1 ratio for minor thirds.

The idea of combining a moderately strict structure with decorative elements of a freer kind is one that Davies could have got from many different sources, but in this case the stimulus was provided, as in the third movement of the Sinfonia, by the 'Sonata sopra Sancta Maria' from the Monteverdi Vespers. As the adagio proceeds, so the ornaments around the cantus become more numerous and more diverse in their harmonic references, until the climax is reached in the subsection of E♭. The note A, consistently locked in its original octave placement up to this point, suddenly leaps up three octaves (bar 48) to become the highest pitch in the whole adagio and also the loudest, marked *fff*. As in the ground idea, the achievement of the peak is followed by a much swifter descent, and in the final subsection each note has returned to its original register.

In amplifying the ground idea, the adagio has, despite the characteristic preponderance of wide intervals throughout much of its course, made clear the mode of the work and other fixed aspects of its harmony: the favouring of 'modulations' into transpositions of the mode upwards by its own intervals of a major second, a minor third, a perfect fourth, a diminished fifth and a diminished seventh; and the functioning of A as main pivot with E♭, its tritonal opposite, as subsidiary pivot. These harmonic features obviously result from the choice of *Ave Maria—Hail Blessed Flower* as source material, in the same way that Davies more commonly uses plainsong fragments, and so it is not surprising that the Quartet should have something in common with more straightforwardly modal works like the *O Magnum Mysterium* carols, where again the flattened third, fifth and seventh were prominent, and where the flattened fifth served as a kind of dominant. It differs, of course, in matters of interval size and also in modulating much more freely and rapidly, especially in the faster music which follows the adagio.

The passage from slow to fast harmonic movement is accentuated by the two-fold repetition in a bar of acceleration

38   accented.

(bar 67) of the minor third A—C with which the adagio had ended, as if this fragment were being whipped up to higher speed in order to usher in a whole new world of exploration. Again the music is based on the mode of the *Ave Maria* carol, and again the harmony is pinned to an underlying traverse along the germinal idea, as follows:

A   Moderato, bars 67–74, followed by Più mosso cadence to
G   Moderato, bars 77–82
B   Più mosso, bars 83–93
✓ C   Allegro, bars 94–132
A $\flat$ = 88, bars 133–44, pivot sustained throughout
C $\flat$ = 88, bars 145–8, pivot sustained throughout
E♭ $\flat$ = 88, bars 149–52, pivot sustained throughout
D $\flat$ = 88, bars 153–4, pivot sustained throughout
B $\flat$ = 88, bars 155–6, pivot sustained throughout
A   Allegro moderato, bars 157—end

There are three main sections, first a fast one (Moderato—Allegro) in which melodic motifs from the ground idea are developed, then a slow one in which the cantus foundation appears in long values, and finally a quick, simple allegro. It will be evident from the résumé above that the decline from the E♭ peak back to A is, as in the ground idea itself and in the adagio, much more rapid than the climb to the dominant, emphasizing the correspondence between the latter part of the work and the opening adagio. Thus, in a very typical manner, the Quartet follows two forms at the same time: on the one hand it compresses four movements into a continuous slow-fast-slow-fast pattern, and on the other it goes through the same harmonic process consecutively in two different ways, first as an adagio and then as something distinctly approximating to a scherzo and trio.

A further quotation, from the opening of the moderato, may help to show how Davies's harmonic methods work in more detail:

The first bar here is that in which the A—C motif is speeded up, and the D♯ in the bass (enharmonic dominant of the mode on A) serves to strengthen the feeling of modality. The melody remains in the same mode throughout the first three bars, but the bass moves to hint at related harmonic areas, and then in

40

the fourth bar leaps down to suggest the mode on B ('dominant' F) while the melody is in the mode on G ('dominant' Db), which should properly be, following the ground idea, the next region to be visited. The ambiguity is settled in favour of the G mode at the start of the next bar, which also sees a modulation to the mode on F ('dominant' Cb). Then the melody moves to the mode on Db while the harmony prepares for a return to the mode on A, fully achieved in the last dotted quaver of bar 74.

A more subtle analysis of the whole Quartet would show how Davies is as dexterous in his harmonic thinking as one would expect were he composing with more normal harmonic means. Even so, the structure becomes most easy to comprehend when the writing is more nearly thematic, as it is in the ensuing allegro. As mentioned above, this passage is basically in the mode on C, and the first melodic line (distinguished as throughout the allegro by normal playing against pizzicato or sul ponticello in the accompaniment) is recognizably akin to the transposition of the ground idea in that mode:

Also to be noted here is the maintenance of the interval-rhythm correspondences from the adagio, as again in the second melodic unit, which is in the 'dominant' (mode on Gb/F#), but with the melodic contour turned inside-out, the repeated C remaining where it is while the other pictures are mostly shunted to opposite sides of this axis:

There are six more melodic units before this part of the section ends at bar 122 (to be followed by a kind of précis and harmonic stocktaking), and in each of them the repeated C remains in place while the original shapes are bent into inversion, retrograde and retrograde inversion forms.

The final allegro moderato, though it marks a return to the home mode on A, is far from affirmative and conclusive. At this point the four instruments are for the first time muted, and there is a sort of boxed-in march, ironically simple, before the work trails away with glances at all those harmonic areas (i.e. transpositions of the mode on to other degrees) that have not been visited. It is wholly characteristic of Davies that he should finish a work of such achievement with a twist of irony and new questioning.

2 AROUND TAVERNER

As a closely argued development, cast in the most hallowed of musical genres and referring to the standard forms, Davies's String Quartet sets itself within the great European tradition. But at the same time, by virtue of its inward concentration and its peculiarly English aloofness from contemporary continental practice, it looks back to the instrumental music of the sixteenth and seventeenth centuries, and it was to this repertory that Davies turned his attention immediately after the group of works based on the Monteverdi Vespers.

Since 1956 he had been considering an opera on what was then known of the life of John Taverner (c. 1495–1545), a project which would have been encouraged while he was in Cirencester by the presence of the Parish Church of St. John the Baptist, whose magnificent nave, site of the first performance of *O Magnum Mysterium*, is exactly contemporary with Taverner's music. However that may be, the last work he composed in Cirencester was a deliberate preparation for the opera, the First Fantasia on an In Nomine of John Taverner for orchestra (1962). This In Nomine, an instrumental arrangement of the Benedictus from Taverner's *Gloria Tibi Trinitas* mass, had been included in the *Mulliner Book*, and had initiated a curious form of polyphonic instrumental music practised by English composers up to the time of Purcell, often under the same title. Davies's orchestral fantasia can be regarded as an unusually elaborate modern appendage to the repertory, for like his

43

predecessors he uses Taverner's music and the *Gloria Tibi Trinitas* plainsong on which it is based. Work on the opera, *Taverner*, the biggest In Nomine of them all, then followed at Princeton, where Davies also wrote his Second Fantasia on John Taverner's In Nomine for orchestra (1964) and some of the Seven In Nomine for wind quintet, harp and string quartet (1963–4), which interleave arrangements of the Taverner original and of derivatives by John Bull and William Blitheman with new contributions to the genre.

The First Taverner Fantasia reveals, by comparison with Davies's previous full orchestral work, *Prolation*, how far he had travelled during the Cirencester years. The much divided polyphony of Webern and Nono is replaced by a more conventional handling of the orchestra, with the strings carrying the main musical burden. Moreover, even more than in the String Quartet, the argument uses clear harmonic means to achieve a broadly traditional form: indeed, the work has as its groundplan that of a sonata-allegro, with repeated exposition, development, recapitulation and coda, all this coming as the last in a sequence of Chinese boxes, preceded by the *Gloria Tibi Trinitas* chant and then the Taverner In Nomine. Davies's music follows directly upon the latter, with two trumpets recasting the earlier composer's treble incipit, which is given a further twist and inverted to provide the strings with a principal theme for a development-introduction which precedes the sonata movement proper. The harmonies of this section, including most prominently an important whole-tone chord of two superimposed major thirds, D—F♯—E—G♯, are surveyed in a recitative for wind, and then the sonata exposition begins with a reference back to the trumpet duet. The development, or rather decoration, of the exposition leads up to a climactic second recitative, with solo brass sounding through a whole-tone chord on strings, whirling woodwind and the salutations of handbells (often to be heard again in Davies's music at moments of elevation). There is then a long drawn-out coda which ends with the handbells referring directly back to the Taverner on B♭, which, with the D suggested both by the Taverner and the plainsong, is one of the main tonal centres of the work.

As in the Quartet, however, the final page is not a completion but an upbeat leading to future works which would themselves show the same mistrust of strong conclusion; for the split between form and content widens in the Seven In Nomine (see note, p. 139) and becomes part of the stuff of the immense musical argument that is the Second Taverner Fantasia (see note, p. 141), a single-movement symphony four times the length of its predecessor. Again like the Quartet, the Seven In Nomine end with music that wraps up the discussion but also hints at great tracts of territory left unexplored, while the bizarre instrumentation, particularly in the Blitheman arrangement and Davies's own six-part canon, looks forward to many later grotesques and marks the clearest expression so far of a tension between substance and appearance. The canon is a masterpiece of artifice in which the subject is presented against retrograde, inversion and retrograde inversion forms, some of these in their own metres: the final section, for instance, has the same rhythm proceeding simultaneously in triplet crotchet, crotchet and minim units. Yet the shrill instrumentation and strident doublings at fifth or twelfth turn the whole thing into some weird toy mechanism.

The Second Taverner Fantasia, though occasionally producing an incipit of the *Gloria Tibi Trinitas* plainsong or of Taverner's treble line, is much less obviously connected with the In Nomine material than are its predecessors. Composed with some segments from the first act of the opera and containing others that were to serve in the second, it could be regarded as a *Taverner* symphony, but it also relates to the First Fantasia as a further instalment of the process there begun, a fourth in the row of developing structures. It begins with material which has already gained a history, for its starting ideas are transformed variants of Taverner's played by a solo string quartet: the first of them, for example, begins as a transposed inversion of the Taverner treble, D—F—E—D becoming E♭—C—D♭—E♭, and then, where the Taverner continues with a falling whole-tone scale, D—C—Bb, the Davies theme surveys another tonally ambiguous element, the diminished seventh chord, Eb—Gb—C—A. This theme is very clearly present in the succeeding orchestral development (Davies's Section 2) and remains a subject of discussion, albeit in diverse transformed shapes, throughout the 'first movement' (Davies's Sections 1–6), though another powerfully significant feature here is the chord D—F♯—E—G♯ taken up from the First Fantasia and the Seven In Nomine.

The central portion of the Second Fantasia (Davies's Sections 8–10) is regarded by the composer as a scherzo and trio, but it can also be viewed as two linked sets of variations separated by a prestissimo interlude. The variation character is especially marked in the second set, where the first violins lead eight dynamic melodic statements separated by brief passages dominated in turn by harp and double bassoon. Each of the melodies begins with a seventh, and the impression is of different costumes being tried on in a determined search for the right fit. Then, when the final adagio begins, again with a melody opening from a seventh, it seems that the true form has at last been found. Settled into the cellos in a low register and at a slow tempo, the new melody seems indisputably a sign of homecoming, and it starts, moreover, with the very same notes that had served to begin the adagio of the String Quartet.

Then again, the music here looks back quite directly to a more distant precedent, that of Mahler. Stephen Pruslin has suggested parallels between the Second Fantasia and Mahler's Ninth Symphony; Stephen Arnold has pointed to links between the adagio of the Davies work and that of Mahler's Tenth; and the composer himself has been reported by Christopher Ford as remarking that his piece owes much to Mahler's Third. Confusing as it may seem, all of these connections can be observed. Like Mahler's Third Symphony, the fantasia begins with an enormous sonata-allegro, continues with a sequence of shorter movements and ends with an adagio and, like the adagio of the Tenth, Davies's adagio reaches its climax with massive dissonant chords, in this case whole-tone chords. There are even at some moments hints of the F♯

tonality of the Mahler movement. And, as Pruslin points out, Davies is specially Mahlerian in finding it necessary to make the grand musical statement and simultaneously, at the moment of its creation, to attack and question with irony and distortion.

It is in the final adagio that irony becomes most insidious, though it has already been fully apparent in such details as the passage in Section 8 where the exaggerated vibrato of a solo violinist cheapens a theme which is none other than one of the work's foundation stones, the *Gloria Tibi Trinitas* plainsong. There is a similar bathos in the third of the adagio's four main sections, each essentially a restatement of the original melody, for at this point the earnest expressive body of string tone is overlaid by nauseatingly sweet glissandos in the first violins: what in Mahler is a genuine inflective device becomes separated from the main musical structure and made into a tawdry decoration which must cast doubt on the value of what lies beneath. And the adagio's final trick is still more devastating. After the climax, the strings and horns die away to silence as the melody is announced once more by a solo clarinet, with all its emotional load shrugged off. The expressive nuances are reduced to a uniform *pppp*; the grand surge of strings is replaced by the plain amble of a single woodwind instrument at double tempo; and, of course, all the harmonic support is withdrawn. In retrospect, therefore, an enormous question mark is appended to the work immediately after what had appeared to be its most feeling and final achievement. It is a gesture that betokens a crisis of confidence in the principles of large-scale musical construction that Davies had been carefully assembling during the previous decade, a crisis that had, however, been inevitable ever since the negations of the Trumpet Sonata and the gestures of incompletion at the ends of such works as the String Quartet.

The same questioning of the mainsprings of creation, artistic and universal, is at the heart of the opera, *Taverner*. Following the account of Taverner's life given by Edward Fellowes in his introduction to the first volume of *Tudor Church Music*, but now known to be erroneous, the opera casts the composer as a man who, on his conversion to Protestantism, turns into a fanatical persecutor of the Catholic Church, abandons music and even decries his earlier creative accomplishments. His transformation from musician into zealot is sealed at the very moment when he makes this denial in the words given him in Foxe's *Book of Martyrs*: 'I repent me very much that I have made songs to Popish ditties in the time of my blindness.' Words which, at least in modern usage, indicate a horrifying new blindness to his own worth on the part of a man whose great festal mass *Gloria Tibi Trinitas* is quoted and otherwise woven into the musical fabric throughout the opera.

The work is, however, concerned with Taverner not only as artist but as man. The choice of a composer as central figure is obviously useful; but in his thoughts and actions he presents us with questions of more general significance. On one level he is the child who must establish his own way of life having reacted against his parental background (the Church of Rome). Most deeply his case is that of anyone who presumes to question venerated authority and so finds himself with no sure moral precepts, no secure means of distinguishing the noble promptings of conscience from the base impulses of self-interest and inhumanity. Musically and dramatically there can be no resolution of these matters in the opera, for to provide an answer would be to assume the role of prophet or seer, to presume a monopoly of truth which the work itself denies to anyone.

Taverner unfolds in two acts, each of four scenes. Act I, Scene I shows the composer on trial for heresy before the White Abbot: the time is before the beginning of the English Reformation, and Taverner is accused of leanings towards Lutheranism. The evidence against him is marshalled in arias by his father, Richard Taverner (an invented character given the name of an English Erasmian), his wife, Rose Parrowe, a corrupt priest and a boy of his choir. Richard Taverner says in his son's defence that 'his music is witness that he believes', but the whole opera, in making pervasive references to the music in the most diverse circumstances, questions whether this is so, not because Davies accepts the view that creative acts need have no relation to the personality, but rather because of the

48

Gunnie Moberg

Peter Maxwell Davies outside his croft on Hoy

Artricia

Davies with the Fires of London

Stuart Robinson

The Royal Opera House production of *Taverner*, Act I, Scene IV

Keith McMillan/Boosey and Hawkes

William Pearson and the Fires of London in *Eight Songs for a Mad King*

connection already noted between musical and theological cogitation. The first straightforward appearance of a musical idea by Taverner, once more the treble incipit from his In Nomine, comes at the moment when he is disputing the truth of transubstantiation: his music is thus not 'witness that he believes' but rather witness that these things matter to him profoundly, and that through music he explores their meaning. A polyphonic setting of a plainsong melody, such as Taverner conducts in his *Gloria Tibi Trinitas* mass, is not theologically neutral or merely decorative: it takes the given truths and subjects them to adjustment, even to inversion. And when Davies's Taverner refers to his *Gloria Tibi Trinitas* mass in casting doubt on the real presence, the choice of that particular work is by no means arbitrary, for nothing could be more exquisitely pointed than the composition of a mass, to adorn the celebration of Christ present at one place and time, upon the Trinity antiphon which attests the indivisibility of the divine persons throughout all ages.

It is hardly surprising that the Church should always have been suspicious of polyphony, which, under cover of ornamenting the liturgy, allows an individual to voice his own arguments at the most sacred moments of the Church's ritual. Far from being 'but a poor musician', as he is repeatedly described in the opera, Taverner is thus a man who has studied and pondered in his art the most serious religious truths. It follows that the sustained polyphonic argument of Davies's orchestra cannot be accepted as simply support or aural décor. It, too, is concerned with the investigation of truth and meaning, on a level which may rise to interact closely with events on stage, as in the many quotations from the Taverner In Nomine, or remaining as a largely hidden, parallel disputation.

Eventually Taverner is convicted, not for his polyphony but for his more patent heretical views, but he is saved by the intervention of the Cardinal (not named as Wolsey), who is unwilling to lose so skilled a servant. And so in the second scene Taverner is observed continuing his debate with himself while monks, singing intricate canons based on the In Nomine,

49

retail in Latin his past and future life. He considers taking violent action against the Church of Rome, but cannot decide the morality of this and finally places his trust in God. The scene ends with the monks chanting in unchanging octave Ds a prayer for such patience and hope, and then, in one of the work's longer orchestral transitions, the whole developed exposition of the Second Taverner Fantasia is resumed to continue the argument.

The cracked fanfare at the end of that exposition now serves to herald the third scene, between the King (not named as Henry VIII) and the Cardinal. Taverner, of course, is not privy to the councils of the great, and so the orchestra, which has been carrying the burden of his thought, falls silent: the scene is accompanied only by a consort of viols and lute, picking out a complex fabric made up from elements of pavane, galliard and march in Davies's own harmonic style. The King, cynically invoking conscience as his guide, sees a break with Rome as the way to rid himself of an unwanted wife, establish his mistress as Queen and increase his power over the Church. The Cardinal temporizes, and the Jester, the only other character present, ironically draws attention to the self-seeking motives of both parties.

The Jester remains on stage for the fourth scene, revealing himself now as Death and calling forth Taverner, and the orchestra, once more. Taverner recognizes his interrogator, upon which there sounds for the first time the D—F♯—E—G♯ chord from the two fantasias and the Seven In Nomine, which henceforth will be the leitmotiv of the Jester as Death. This enigmatic figure at once challenges Taverner to confess, and confuses him as to his ability to tell good from evil. Two monks appear, one in black and the other in white, the first eventually showing himself as human when the second reveals the features of a monster. 'Wherever Christ is,' sings the first, 'there are Judas, Pilate and the whole Passion': goodness carries with it its antithesis, which may even be indiscernible from it. Death then presses his advantage by a show of the mountain of superstitious, magical accretions to Christianity, relics and the rest, exciting a burst of outrage from his victim. Antichrist

50

appears as an ape in pope's vestments, and Taverner violently denounces Rome. But this is not enough: he must also, Death demands, deny his humanity and his art, and to secure this the interrogator calls upon Richard Taverner and Rose Parrowe. Rose nearly persuades him that he should be content to compose and should not seek to reason out the meaning of his work, and so Death summons his last, crudest but most efficacious trick. A cart is trundled on, led by treble demons and set up for a street Passion play. Death mounts the Cross as Joking Jesus, and his pitifully inadequate portrayal of the Saviour hits home by the power of emotion: Taverner resolves that he must take up the sword against Rome on behalf of this Lord. The demons drag the cart and props away while singing a piping, thoroughly debased setting of 'Atollite portas', the last text from the Five Motets, and Taverner signs his confession. Then, accompanied only by a solo violin and deep bell sounds in an ominous slow tempo, Death states the present evacuated, possessed case of the composer, and Taverner, as the music becomes more animated though crude in its woodwind scoring, excitedly voices his enthusiasm for his newfound faith, his determination to 'defend Christ's faith with the sword and the fire, for love of Him'. Death shrieks a mock salutation.

The opera's second act begins as a nightmare parody of the first. Act II, Scene I is again set in the courtroom, but now Taverner is the judge-inquisitor and the White Abbot the accused, for with Taverner's conversion the English Reformation has happened. The witnesses are the same; the music, however, is speeded up, simplified and curtailed, so that the trial proceeds helter-skelter to the sentencing of the Abbot to be burned at the stake. Then, at the point where Taverner had been reprieved at the instigation of the Cardinal, the latter enters again, but his power has vanished: he has no face. Death is shown in control of the Wheel of Fortune, upon which is indicated the rise and fall of princes, and the chorus vehemently point the opera's central question: 'But who shall know St. Michael, who the Serpent?'

Act II, Scene II is another audience between King and

Cardinal, again accompanied by renaissance instruments. This time, however, the ensemble is of winds and percussion, and the earlier renaissance–modern fusion is replaced by a sequence of imitations in early styles corrupted by modernisms: dances for ensemble and plainsong elaborations for regal or positive organ. As in his *Shakespeare Music* for an ensemble of modern instruments (1964), Davies shows great skill and invention in the writing of pastiches of particular pieces or styles, but the bite of parody is sharper in the opera. Moving in time from the early sixteenth century to the early seventeenth, the 'points and dances' shadow the progress of the Reformation in England, and this is unfolded also in the stage action, the Cardinal being rerobed by the Jester as an Anglican Archbishop. The Jester/Death figure has already shown himself in control of human destinies; he is now seen also to puppeteer the Church, while monarch and cleric discuss the progress of the royal marriage, the denial of Rome and the dissolution of the monasteries.

Corresponding to Act I, Scene II, Act II, Scene III is again set in the chapel, where now the White Abbot and his monks are saying mass to a text drawn from the liturgies for Maundy Thursday and Good Friday, texts filled with references to the betrayal of Christ by Judas. Taverner enters at a point which identifies him with the traitorous disciple, and while the mass continues he states the standard party line about the need for a reformation of the religious houses because of their corruption. When he recalls his own shame at having once contributed to that corruption, 'providing the furniture', a solo viola lets loose a quotation from his In Nomine in inversion and tritone transposition, utterly negated. But his denial of his art is to be yet more dramatically presented. At the moment of elevation, soldiers enter the chapel to dispossess the monks, and their captain pours the consecrated wine on to the floor. Taverner stands by as this happens, and even as the monks depart singing the Benedictus in the setting from his *Gloria Tibi Trinitas* mass. Gradually surrounded by the—at first—accommodating but then insidious sounds of Davies's own music, the Taverner Benedictus dies away pathetically for the transition to the final scene, that of the White Abbot's execution.

This immense choral-orchestral tableau draws together the harmonic threads of the whole opera, and in particular its emphasis on tonal centres taken from the diminished seventh chord D—F—A♭—B. The whole second half of the scene is played out over the adagio from the Second Taverner Fantasia, this underpinning the White Abbot's final warning, in which he foresees a time when there will be no need of the fire to dispose of heretics, a time when social pressures would have become strong enough for dissenting thought to be inconceivable, or else laughable. The nihilist woodwind codetta now rises beneath Taverner's last words, a prayer for divine assistance, and there is no need for the lines which conclude the first edition of the libretto but have been omitted in the finished opera: 'The heathen are sunk down in the pit that they made: In the net which they hid is their own foot taken.' For it is all too clear that Taverner has destroyed himself. Offstage recorders playing his In Nomine at this point add a deep melancholy irony, and the other overlay on the music of the Second Fantasia, a solo cello alluding to an Easter plainsong, may be a sign of the resurrection of Antichrist, to be acted out in another work, as much as a shred of hope vouchsafed.

By the time he completed *Taverner*, in 1968, Davies had written several other works, many of them emerging from the musical, theological and psychological substance of the opera. For instance, *Veni Sancte Spiritus* (1963), composed for an American high school choir with accompaniment for a small percussionless orchestra, shares some of the opera's harmonic features, ending with a unison D. Moreover, as a setting not only of the hymn but of the Vulgate Pentecost narrative, it too is concerned with a spiritual presence in man, though without the opera's doubts as to the nature of that presence. And *The Shepherd's Calendar* for voices and large instrumental gathering (1965), a schools' piece more in the manner of *O Magnum Mysterium* than the relatively difficult and severely Stravinskyan *Veni Sancte Spiritus*, is again concerned with the arrival of the divine in the world. After the coming of spring has been joyously and lengthily welcomed to texts from the Goliard poets, a solo treble sings a text from an Advent vespers, 'The Lord will come and not be slow', and the work ends again in D, this time with chords of D major. It also, in combining nature with Christian mythology, points the way to Davies's much later association with George Mackay Brown.

But his most important choral work of this period, and the one most intimately connected with the matter of *Taverner*, was *Ecce Manus Tradentis* for voices and nonet (1964), a motet on the betrayal of Christ. The text, again taken from the Vulgate, consists of Gospel passages relating Christ's consecration of the bread and wine at the Last Supper and his foretelling of his betrayal, then Peter's denial, and finally Judas's act of betrayal in kissing his Master. Most of the words are delivered as a slow chordal chant in sombre harmony which has its roots in the 'Death chord' from *Taverner*, and which shows tendencies all through the piece to slip into the casual, easy D minor that steals in at the end beneath the solo soprano's ecstatic high-flung announcement of Judas's sweet crime. This last solo line is the one moment of musical generosity in a score whose stark frigidity is enhanced by the rhythmic evenness, most unusual in Davies, and the instrumentation for wind, handbells and harp, this ensemble providing a development in meditative interludes and lugubrious polyphony underneath the generally static choral pronouncements. It is, Davies has said, the bleakest piece he has written.

INTERLUDE: ANTECHRIST

Antechrist (1967), scored for piccolo, bass clarinet, violin, cello and three percussionists, was the first work Davies wrote for the Pierrot Players, and so it opened a new period in his output. But at the same time it has connections with *Taverner*, then nearing completion, as the composer has acknowledged (see note, p. 144). The title does not refer, however, to the ape-faced pope who makes a cameo appearance in Act I, Scene IV of the opera, nor to the arch-deceiver of John's letters. Instead Davies is here concerned with a figure from medieval sub-Christian mythology, a spiritual Antichrist who is barely distinguishable from the real Christ and yet who embodies a total reversal of Christian precepts: he is the spirit of negation implicitly present in the same scene of *Taverner*, the lord whom the protagonist comes to serve in believing himself to be following the will of God. And the musical means for depicting at once identity and inversion had also come in *Taverner*, for they are those of parody.

Parody in the technical sense—the method used by medieval and renaissance composers to create, say, a mass from a motet—had, of course, been an important feature of Davies's music since *Alma Redemptoris Mater*. What was new in *Taverner* was the use of parody in the more common sense of distortion to render something ludicrous or grotesque. As has been noted, the whole second act of the opera is a parody of the first, and the points and dances of Act II, Scene II parody period pieces. Moreover, the meaning of Antichrist as the presiding spirit of parody in Davies's mind was confirmed by a concert given by the Fires of London in 1973 under the title 'The Triumph of Antichrist', the programme including not only *Antechrist* itself but 'a series of images which are "infiltrated" or "corrupted" from within'.

The image corrupted in *Antechrist* is a thirteenth-century motet, *Deo Confitemini—Domino*, which is taken bodily into the piece as its first section. This was the first time that Davies had made such a large-scale quotation within his music, and it was perhaps to minimize the stylistic dichotomy that he chose a medieval work which is already very curious harmonically and also, following the practice of the Seven In Nomine, brought it into his own musical world by his strident, disjunct instrumentation and by octave transpositions which split the lines across a wide range:

As will be clear from this example, which shows the first bars of *Antechrist*, the motet is riven with discords that are redoubled by Davies's doubling of the top line in fourths: the two upper parts are consonant, as are the two lower parts, but the combination of the three is glaringly adrift.

56

After the whole motet has been played, *Antechrist* continues immediately with a stream of new derivations from the medieval material, and the music speeds up in the ratio 11:8 except for two canons on the *Deo Confitemini* treble which restore the tempo of the opening. These are among the piece's several distinct short sections, which run as follows:

1. Arrangement of the *Deo Confitemini—Domino*;
2. Canon for piccolo and violin over bass clarinet cantus;
3. Cello solo with Burmese gongs, other instruments entering later;
4. Variation of 2;
5. *Deo Confitemini* treble in E, in canon with its retrograde, inversion and retrograde inversion;
6. Canon for glockenspiel and cello;
7. Variation of 6 with added cantus on other instruments;
8. Very slow condensation;
9. Further variation of 6;
10. *Deo Confitemini* treble in F$\sharp$, again in canon with its retrograde, inversion and retrograde inversion, but also with internal elaborations and with the inverted parts rhythmically diminished in the ratio 2:3.

Section 2, coming straight after the original motet, emerges from its world at an angle. The piccolo again starts with repeated A and G, the bass clarinet again has a D, and the bass drum increases, absurdly, the emphasis earlier provided by the tabor. However, the new music very swiftly establishes its own identity:

The piccolo–violin pairing is that of the motet treble, but after following this a little way the piccolo pulls away into its own track, continuing down the same whole-tone scale a further two steps (A—G—F—Eb—Db), then going up a minor third instead of down a semitone, and finally imitating its model again by exploring the alternative whole-tone scale (E—D—C—Gb—Ab). In doing so it has used all the chromatic notes but B and Bb, which, given that the *Deo Confitemini* treble is locked into a range from C to A, can be regarded as the boundary pitches of the original.

Meanwhile the violin, whose scooping glissandos are as much a parody gesture as the extreme shrillness of the piccolo, has a considerably altered retrograde of its partner's line, and the section continues with such little reversible duos, each later one introduced by a repeated C on the cowbell in what is a defective imitation of the part for handbells in the motet arrangement. There are also other references to the *Deo Confitemini* to be found in the rhythms, particularly of the piccolo part, which follows the *Ars Antiqua* modality of the motet in using only a small number of different divisions of the

bar 22

basic dotted-note unit: crotchet plus quaver (or vice versa), three semiquavers or two dotted semiquavers. The even values tend to dominate the middle of the section, but at the end there is an exact return in the piccolo to the pattern of Example 8.

This restoration of the rhythmic shape after a process of dissolution is also to be found in the pitch workings, for in each tiny duo the piccolo is progressively transformed so that the final state is an almost exact inversion of the first. The table below, which has to be conjectural in some minor details because of Davies's repetitions and omissions, shows how this happens, with numbers to indicate intervals in semitones (ignoring octave transpositions):

A $\overset{10}{-}$ G $\overset{10}{-}$ F $\overset{10}{-}$ Eb $\overset{10}{-}$ Db $\overset{3}{-}$ Fb $\overset{10}{-}$ D $\overset{10}{-}$ C $\overset{6}{-}$ Gb $\overset{2}{-}$ Ab

G $\overset{10}{-}$ F $\overset{10}{-}$ Eb $\overset{11}{-}$ D $\overset{10}{-}$ C $\overset{3}{-}$ Eb $\overset{10}{-}$ Db $\overset{11}{-}$ C $\overset{4}{-}$ E $\overset{2}{-}$ F#

F $\overset{11}{-}$ E $\overset{10}{-}$ D $\overset{11}{-}$ Db $\overset{10}{-}$ Cb $\overset{3}{-}$ D $\overset{11}{-}$ C# $\overset{11}{-}$ C $\overset{3}{-}$ Eb $\overset{1}{-}$ E

Eb $\overset{11}{-}$ D $\overset{11}{-}$ Db $\overset{0}{-}$ Db $\overset{10}{-}$ B $\overset{3}{-}$ D $\overset{11}{-}$ Db $\overset{11}{-}$ C $\overset{2}{-}$ D $\overset{1}{-}$ Eb

Db $\overset{0}{-}$ Db $\overset{11}{-}$ C $\overset{1}{-}$ Db $\overset{10}{-}$ Cb $\overset{2}{-}$ Db $\overset{0}{-}$ Db $\overset{11}{-}$ C $\overset{1}{-}$ Db $\overset{0}{-}$ Db

Fb : line omitted

D $\overset{1}{-}$ Eb $\overset{1}{-}$ Fb $\overset{2}{-}$ Gb $\overset{10}{-}$ Fb $\overset{11}{-}$ Eb $\overset{1}{-}$ Fb $\overset{0}{-}$ Fb $\overset{11}{-}$ Eb $\overset{0}{-}$ Eb

C $\overset{1}{-}$ Db $\overset{1}{-}$ D $\overset{2}{-}$ E $\overset{0}{-}$ E $\overset{11}{-}$ Eb $\overset{2}{-}$ F $\overset{0}{-}$ F $\overset{9}{-}$ D $\overset{11}{-}$ C#

F# $\overset{2}{-}$ G# $\overset{1}{-}$ A $\overset{2}{-}$ B $\overset{0}{-}$ B $\overset{11}{-}$ Bb $\overset{2}{-}$ C $\overset{1}{-}$ C# $\overset{7}{-}$ G# $\overset{11}{-}$ G

Ab $\overset{2}{-}$ Bb $\overset{2}{-}$ C $\overset{2}{-}$ D $\overset{2}{-}$ E $\overset{9}{-}$ C# $\overset{2}{-}$ Eb $\overset{2}{-}$ F $\overset{6}{-}$ B $\overset{10}{-}$ A

Each new transformation starts on the next note of the original set, and the stepwise reduction then expansion of intervals naturally generates a closing in towards repetition, which is especially marked in the form beginning on Db, followed by an opening out. In the piccolo presentation of this process, the lines are read alternately forwards and backwards (i.e. beginning on A, then on F#, then on F, and so on), which rather disguises the nature of the transformation, and the penultimate

B is flattened, so that the inversion is not quite perfect. However, the movement towards monotony and back again is obvious, and the final form declares its kinship with the first not only in its rhythm but also in its contour: in its essence it is an inversion, but in outward show it is the same. It is, therefore, a perfect image of Antichrist.

The agent of this transformation of principle into anti-principle is implicitly the bass clarinet melody which lies beneath in long notes, and which turns out to be a précis of the *Gloria Tibi Trinitas* plainsong, D—F—D—C—D—F—G—D—E—C—D. This would have a place in the work by virtue of the D-centred mode it shares with the *Deo Confitemini* and also of its prominence in Davies's musical mind at this time, but there is a deeper reason for it to be drawn into play here. The text of the *Deo Confitemini* is concerned with the incarnation of Christ, which The Trinitarian antiphon would seem to deny, and indeed the music of the motet might appear already to be questioning its verbal message, with its three parts and its bottom voice littered with what can be conceived as references to the *Gloria Tibi Trinitas* chant. On this level, therefore, *Antechrist* is a meditation on the mystery of the Trinity begun by the thirteenth-century composer.

The two basic materials, motet and plainsong antiphon, begin to interfere with each other more directly later in the piece. For example, in Section 7 the piccolo has a cantus in long values, A—E—F—E♭—C♯—D—A, which is obtained by subtracting the intervals of the *Gloria Tibi Trinitas* from those of the piccolo's first *Deo Confitemini* derivative, that of Example 8:

$$A \xrightarrow{10} G \xrightarrow{10} F \xrightarrow{10} E♭ \xrightarrow{10} D♭ \xrightarrow{3} F♭ \xrightarrow{10} D \xrightarrow{10} C$$
$$D \xrightarrow{3} F \xrightarrow{9} D \xrightarrow{0} D \xrightarrow{0} D \xrightarrow{10} (C) \xrightarrow{2} D \xrightarrow{3} F$$
$$A \xrightarrow{7} E \xrightarrow{1} F \xrightarrow{10} E♭ \xrightarrow{10} C♯ \xrightarrow{\quad 1 \quad} D \xrightarrow{7} A$$

One may very well not notice exactly what is going on here, but there is no difficulty in observing that the piccolo has always hitherto been associated with the *Deo Confitemini* treble, whether in quotation (Section 1), derivative forms (Sections 2 and 4) or reversal (Section 5), whereas now it takes on the cantus role of the bass clarinet in Section 2.

The final section of the piece, the double mensural canon on the *Deo Confitemini* treble, seems on the surface a return again to the music's secure medieval foundations, but there are alarming signs that all is not well. The piccolo once more takes the treble, but with some smoothening of the rhythm and, near the end, stabs at the extreme top of its range. Moreover, it is doubled by the glockenspiel, which not only plays in a different metre but also adds decorations referring back to the transformations it has assumed in previous sections. Similarly, the violin and the cello allow their music to be cheapened by the glissandos of Sections 2–4, and the bass clarinet indulges in octave transpositions to make a jagged line out of the inversion of the thirteenth-century melody. And though the canon still manages to remain decisively in F♯, there is a final twist upwards, and in the last bar harmonic security is suddenly withdrawn as the fifth F♯—C♯ slides to the tritone G♯—D.

This has the effect of leaving the piece on a thoroughly upsetting upbeat, even though the last chord can be seen as completing a whole-tone progression through the sections based directly on the *Deo Confitemini* treble from D (1) to E (5) to F♯ (10) and finally G♯. For that progression covers the ground of the 'Death chord' from *Taverner*, outlined in Antichrist's final victorious tritone. As the opera made manifest, to follow Antichrist is spiritual death, and yet to ignore the existence of negation is to indulge in self-deception, perhaps the ultimate betrayal.

3 PARODY AND MUSIC THEATRE

The existence of the Pierrot Players, coupled with the completion of *Taverner* in 1968, released in Davies a torrent of creative energy to be poured into the composition of three important works of music theatre—*Missa Super l'Homme Armé* (1968, revised in 1971), *Eight Songs for a Mad King* (1969) and *Vesalii Icones* (also 1969)—along with other works for the new ensemble and a pair of orchestral scores, *Worldes Blis* (1966–9) and *St. Thomas Wake* (1969). But perhaps the most significant trigger in producing this outburst was another work dating from the *Taverner* years though not performed until 1968, *Revelation and Fall* for soprano and sixteen players (1966). Here, in setting a prose poem by Trakl, Davies faced the need to re-experience the savagery, the dislocation and the sense of catastrophe that inform so much of the art of the few years before the First World War, and, as it now seems inevitably, it was to Schoenberg, especially to *Pierrot Lunaire*, that he turned for the means to cope.

By contrast with the largely syllabic, declamatory style of vocal writing in *Taverner*, the singer's part in *Revelation and Fall* is an extraordinary virtuoso assault, requiring a range of almost three octaves, several different kinds of delivery, and the ability to negotiate complex rhythms and rapid, jagged melismas. The aim is to articulate the shriek of desperation in the Trakl text, yet at the same time the music does everything in its power to stave off the point at which that shriek becomes

62

inevitable. If it had not done so, then the whole thing might have collapsed into incoherence and banality, against which Davies, like Schoenberg in *Pierrot Lunaire*, fights with the weapons of compositional artifice. To quote his own remarks from the score, the work 'represents a marked extension, in comparison with my earlier works in the use of late medieval/renaissance composition techniques ... in the complexity of rhythmic relationships between simultaneous "voices", in the use of cantus firmus with long melismas branching out, and in the use of mensural canon'. Not only that, but it is also securely structured as a piece of thoroughly developing chamber music, being in this respect even more traditional than such a work as the String Quartet. After the introductory sequence, which ends with a little 'chorale-canon', there is a long purely instrumental allegro in which Davies applies his technique of progressive thematic distortion. Moreover, the distinct segments of the work are carefully bound together by thematic links involving plainsong ideas, and there is even a wholesale recapitulation, albeit with the original vocal line reassigned to wind soloists (bars 265–303, cf. bars 137–74). The strenuous seriousness of the music, which is ironically twisted but by no means undermined when the band slips towards dance music at the voice's invocation 'O bitterer Tod', creates a context in which the soprano's most extreme outburst, screamed into a loudhailer, can come as a real shock though it is also a real necessity, all other avenues of expression having been explored.

Indeed, the terror of *Revelation and Fall* is sufficiently well established musically to justify the quasi-theatrical presentation Davies has preferred, with the soprano appearing in blood-red nun's habit to act the part of Trakl's 'Sister'. However, it was only in the works of 1968–9 that he was to take full advantage of the concert hall as theatre. In *Missa Super l'Homme Armé* (see note, p. 145) the vocal soloist, singer or actor, is again a religious, though vested in robes belonging to the opposite sex as an outward mark of the whole work's *Antechrist*-like inversion of meaning. However, it should be noted that the work was in its first version not a dramatic piece, the words being delivered by a boy's voice on tape, and in that version it was more nearly an extrovert cousin to *Ecce Manus Tradentis*, whose text in both versions it largely shares. What is new in *Missa Super l'Homme Armé* is, therefore, not the subject matter, which is again spiritual betrayal, but the range and vividness of the musical imagery that *Antechrist* had made possible.

Working, as it were, inside the Agnus Dei from an anonymous unfinished *L'Homme Armé* mass, Davies uses all the parody techniques of *Antechrist* and more to distort the original into unexpected directions. There are the same parody gestures—the inappropriate and exaggerated expressive effects, the unbalanced textures and the extreme registers—joined by parody imitations, when the material is bent into the mould of a baroque trio sonata, or a sentimental Victorian hymn, or a foxtrot, and the appearance of these musical mockeries, which unlike the dances of *Taverner* or *Shakespeare Music* are viciously loaded and quite out of place, is profoundly disturbing. It is, of course, equally disturbing to conventional religious feeling that a parody hymn, already placed under suspicion in being allotted to the harmonium, should be associated with Judas's betrayal, and that Christ's curse on the traitor should be exclaimed by a transvestite nun who should 'at the end of the piece foxtrot out, perhaps pulling off his wimple'. Yet by no means is *Missa Super l'Homme Armé* a cheap exercise in blasphemy. The questions it raises are those of discerning and communicating religious truth, and in particular of distinguishing what is true from its precise opposite: questions which had been raised but not resolved in *Taverner* and other works, and which were to be examined again still more searchingly in *Vesalii Icones*. At the same time, the ninefold structure of *Missa Super l'Homme Armé*, a feature also of the virtuoso clarinet piece, *Hymnos* (1967), and the sextet, *Stedman Caters* (1968, see note, p. 135), suggests that the source of difficulty may still be the Trinity-Incarnation paradox of *Taverner* and *Antechrist*.

Since *Missa Super l'Homme Armé* became a theatre piece only in 1971, *Eight Songs for a Mad King* (see note, p. 147) must

64

Nicolette Hallett

Mary Thomas in *Miss Donnithorne's Maggot*

Gunnie Moberg/Boosey and Hawkes

Neil Mackie (Magnus) and Michael Rippon (Herald of Earl Magnus)
in *The Martyrdom of St. Magnus*

count as Davies's first real work of music theatre. It is also his most spectacular, with the mad king ranting at his caged musicians, and yet this is far from being a Bedlam sideshow to titillate an audience. Nor does the work allow us to congratulate ourselves as superior to the eighteenth century in our gifts of compassion, and in this respect it joins all those other Davies works that reject the easy solution. For the audience at *Eight Songs* has come to be entertained by a show of madness, and the perturbing character of the work is due not merely to its startling depiction of insanity but more to the fact that it obliges us to acknowledge that the madhouse does exert a terrible fascination. And the king's crazed pronouncements would be completely meaningless if they did not sensibly connect with more normal mentality, so that we are not only voyeurs, but voyeurs at our own potential extremity.

The techniques Davies used to create this portrait of madness were developed directly from those of immediately preceding works. The vocalist's part takes on the manic intensity of *Revelation and Fall*, though that work's rhythmic complexity and superabundance of notes are left behind to be replaced by an extraordinary range of over five octaves and a variety of weird effects stimulated by the outlandish virtuosity of Roy Hart. Meanwhile the instrumental music is filled with parodies at many levels, as in *Missa Super l'Homme Armé*, with the difference that a single root source is exchanged for a manifold variety of allusions. This is unusual in Davies's music and so, too, is the degree of liberty allowed in *Eight Songs* to the performers, as if, faced with a rush of strong musical images, the composer had not the opportunity to do anything but dash them down as swiftly as possible.

In doing so he appeals to *Pierrot Lunaire* very much more directly than had been the case in *Revelation and Fall*. Not only does *Eight Songs* grow as music theatre from the possibilities suggested by Schoenberg's work—and indeed embodied in the highly dramatic performances given by Mary Thomas with Davies's group—but the instrumentation this time is closely similar, there is again a duet for voice and flute as third number, and one is again confronted by a character who is undefinable. Where Schoenberg's reciter speaks of Pierrot sometimes in the first and sometimes in the third person, Davies's vocalist identifies himself with King George III but leaves one unsure as to whether the work is intended as a study of that monarch or of a madman who believes himself to be George. Furthermore, Davies takes the gap between voice and instrument in Schoenberg and widens it still further—dramatically by placing the instrumentalists in cages, and musically by providing ensemble material which hardly ever supports the voice but instead proposes a stream of images sparked off by the hysterical vocal line. In the realm of vocal music it is impossible to imagine anything going further, and it is not surprising that in his next theatre piece, *Vesalii Icones* (see note, p. 152), Davies should have chosen a dancer and a cellist as his soloists.

This dual focus is essential in a work that is even denser with simultaneous ambiguities and contradictions than any other in Davies's output, a work that makes use of all the parody techniques he had developed during the preceding two or three years. As his note makes clear, the music is shot through with elements that deride or question, and it also borrows from earlier compositions sharing its concern with the betrayal of Christ, *Ecce Manus Tradentis* and *Missa Super l'Homme Armé*, for indeed this is the theme of the whole work and not just its second number, entitled 'The Betrayal of Christ', containing what Davies calls a 'sickly sweet' melody of feigned adoration.

The choice of the cello, that instrument with a notable history of religiose meditations behind it, becomes particularly significant, since the work is attacking any meretricious betrayal of spiritual thought. Such a betrayal leads to the triumph of Antichrist, who, in rising from Christ's tomb at the end of the work, raises the whole matter of Christ's meaning for the Church. Here, with Kierkegaard, Davies suggests that the Church has since its inception been guilty of Christ's betrayal, worshipping not the Christ of the New Testament but a double who is outwardly similar and inwardly inverted. But, of course, again with Kierkegaard, Davies makes no claims for himself as alternative visionary. If *Vesalii Icones* has a message, it is the dread one that religious truth, though of terrible importance, is beyond the capacity of human beings not only to understand but even to recognize.

It is noteworthy that the triumph of Antichrist comes to the sound of a foxtrot, for during this period the foxtrot was an obsessive image in Davies's music, an image of total corruption. Commercial music is itself a betrayal of all the art's powers to present new, stretching experiences; and the commercial music of the past, having no part in Davies's own life since he was not born until the foxtrot era was in decline, is an invitation to indulge in fake nostalgia, the most unreal of emotions. Yet, and this is wholly characteristic, Davies's foxtrots quite clearly have an awful seductive appeal for the composer as much as for his listeners: otherwise they would hardly occur so frequently and be worked so skilfully. Apart from the examples already noted in *Missa Super l'Homme Armé* and *Vesalii Icones*, there are foxtrots masquerading as pavanes in a pair of Purcell arrangements from 1968 (see note, p. 146). In this case Davies proposed his realizations as expressions of the spirit of the original, but if the material has to be modified so drastically in order that it may have its original effect, then no musical performance can have any claim whatever to authority, and a problem of honesty at the very heart of the art is smilingly exposed.

So it is again in Davies's biggest foxtrot piece, *St. Thomas Wake*, which takes up a foxtrot from *Eight Songs for a Mad King* together with several new ones. Here there is a straight confrontation between commercial music, played by a Thirties band, and serious symphonic argument, assigned to a standard orchestra, with the besetting irony that the latter depends on the catchy numbers of the former, since the two big sequences of orchestral development are concerned with the material announced by the band. And, of course, there is the further irony that both are the work of the same composer, whose judgements of relative worth are not to be easily assumed from the music when each style begs from the other. Once more the means of transformation, and the means by which both orchestra and band draw material from the John

67

Bull pavane that gives the work its title, are those of *Antechrist* on a much larger scale.

Davies's score for the film, *The Devils* (1970, see note, p. 155), included a further foxtrot, but inevitably the voice of popular music is loudest in his other collaboration with Ken Russell, *The Boy Friend* (1971), where he takes Sandy Wilson's Fifties imitations of Twenties numbers and in this act of double pastiche exaggerates the glee to bursting-point. *The Devils*, by contrast, once more presented him with material relating to the corruption of religious truth, and to the flowering of the most extreme corruption within the most intense devotion, spiritual and sexual. This is naturally most explicit in those scenes dealing with Sister Jeanne's passion for Father Grandier, scenes which are the last flaring of a naked expressionism such as no artist has been able to sustain for long: the case of Schoenberg is similar. Though Davies has continued to work in the genre of music theatre, he has generally done so by looking to rather different subject matter, except in the case of *Miss Donnithorne's Maggot* (1974) where he attempts to re-enter the mad world of *Eight Songs* by surer and safer means to speak of the deranged jilted lady who also provided the model for Dickens's Miss Havisham.

More central to his output is *Blind Man's Buff* (1972), an examination of values which gains from the masque-like detachment made possible by his later style. Basing the piece on the final scene of Büchner's comedy, *Leonce und Lena*, he here presents two singing characters, both of them with histories in other works of his: King and Jester. They are both important because they are both images of the artist, who may consider himself the King creating and ruling his own realm of imagination, or the Jester who is a paid entertainer, but who also uniquely has the power to overturn and question accepted meaning. It is hardly insignificant, therefore, that the roles of the two should be inextricably confused in *Blind Man's Buff*. It is the King who opens the piece with a nonsense song and he, too, who kills himself later in absurd pantomime fashion, while the Jester voices a more serious disquiet about matters of identity. He is, moreover, represented not only by a mezzo-soprano (the King is a treble or soprano role) but also by a dancer and a mime, and the whole work is strewn with musical, verbal and choreographic images of reflection and twinning. For instance, after the King's first song the Jester asks himself: 'Am I this, or this, or this, or that?', peeling off successive masks as he does so, with his line doubled by a flute at the tritone but in an inverted contour. And at the very end the two characters merge into each other in an echo song.

Davies's fascination, perhaps his identification, with the figure of the Jester gave rise also at this time to *Fool's Fanfare*, an occasional piece written for a Shakespeare concert and setting fools' speeches from the plays, but still with the sharp bright irony of *Blind Man's Buff*. But by 1978, in *Le Jongleur de Notre-Dame*, the artist-fool has become a member of the community. The work takes up the familiar legend, also the subject of an opera by Massenet, concerning a juggler who has only his circus skills to offer to the Virgin, and who finds his gift graciously accepted. Though intended once more for the Fires of London, it is an entertainment of a much lighter cast than its predecessors. Now the virtuosity of the flautist, the clarinettist and the percussionist is directed into flamboyant solos which are their offerings to the Virgin, so that the use of extreme instrumental possibilities no longer signifies extreme emotional states, as it had in *Eight Songs* and *Vesalii Icones*, but is objectified as gloriously showy technical prowess. When the Virgin, having sat immobile as a statue throughout most of the piece, eventually responds to the juggler with her own brilliant violin solo, the game of instrumental extravagance risks seeming coy, yet the piece does hold on to the naive miracle-play aura reinforced by its ebullient overture and recessional for children's band. It is, however, a success on the terms of Stravinsky's *Renard*, of fable, rather than as previously on the deep psychological terms of *Pierrot Lunaire*, even though the cello projects an intensely passionate line calling back to *Vesalii Icones*.

Le Jongleur also belongs with *Vesalii Icones*, and with *Eight Songs*, as a work created for the Fires of London and exploiting instrumentalists as dramatic figures: caged songbirds in *Eight*

Songs, a wordless but absolutely central presence in *Vesalii Icones*, monks speaking through their instruments in *Le Jongleur*. But this last, written a decade after Davies's earlier essays in the genre, comes from a creative period when he had found some solution to the problems that had arisen in the late Sixties and early Seventies—problems, in particular, of identity. It was not that he had found it difficult to establish his own voice: far from it, even his earliest pieces are quite distinctively his, and by the late Sixties his music had developed a large number of distinguishing features. The parody techniques could belong to nobody else, nor could such recurrent musical images as signals of alarm from whistles and football rattles (in *Eight Songs, St. Thomas Wake*, *Revelation and Fall* and the Purcell realizations) nor, even more frequent, bell sounds, these often having a ritual significance, as in *Vesalii Icones*, but at other times being explored as purely musical phenomena, as in the Five Little Pieces for piano (1960–64). Moreover, Davies's use of his favoured instrumental sextet had quickly become quite personal, particularly in the overload of emotion he could pack into solo string lines with their glissandos and heavy vibrato, or in the cutting virtuosity he drew from Alan Hacker's clarinet, for which he wrote *Hymnos* and revised *Stedman Doubles*. But if he had definitively created a style for what in the *Vesalii Icones* note he calls his '"real" music', then he had no less certainly demonstrated his ability to imitate the styles of anything from a *Mulliner Book* plainsong setting to a foxtrot, a Victorian hymn to a renaissance mass, a Beethoven analysis to a Bach sonata. Someone so skilled in creating masks was obviously in no position to provide guarantees about the genuineness of what he presented as his '"real" music' and of course the quotation marks are an acknowledgement that such a guarantee was lacking.

If it was to come at all, it could come only from within, and it was at the very time when he was producing his most violent expressionist pieces, between *Revelation and Fall* and *Vesalii Icones*, that Davies set out to define his creative self in *Worldes Blis* (see note, p. 149). Like the Second Taverner Fantasia, this is a big symphonic movement in many sections playing continuously for around forty minutes, but it differs from its predecessor in that its whole development is not away from initial ideas but towards a late statement of its basic seed, a thirteenth-century English song on the vanity of earthly contentment. The logical, symmetrical processes of the Second Taverner Fantasia are at the same time replaced by a very much more troubling, restless impulse which carries the music on with great weight into ever newer fields of investigation without allowing old questions to be answered. Furthermore, the orchestral imagery is sometimes of a savagery and force unprecedented except in the works created by Mahler, Schoenberg, Berg and Webern in the years immediately before the First World War, and without successor since, for in this work Davies did find, as his note explains, a mental resting place that eventually found its physical equivalent on Hoy. *Worldes Blis* ends, as does *St. Thomas Wake*, with the *Taverner* 'death chord' to be a sign of questions still hanging, but if nothing is resolved by the music, at least it quietened ghosts and permitted its composer to embark on a quite new phase in his creative career.

INTERLUDE: AVE MARIS STELLA

The two earlier of these interludes were concerned with works that are to some degree transitional, but this is not the case with *Ave Maris Stella* (1975), written at a time when Davies's Orkney period was already well under way. However, in certain respects it was an innovatory piece: it was the first important work Davies composed in his renovated croft looking out from Hoy on to the Pentland Firth, and it was the first work in which he used various structural means that were to make possible the First Symphony and other works of the late Seventies and early Eighties. It might also be described as a retrospectively transitional piece, in that it looks back to the fractured vehemence of the late Sixties when it arrives at the climactic seventh of its nine sections. But, above all, it demands attention as one of Davies's finest, most searching achievements, designed to engage the virtuosity of the Fires instrumentalists on flute, clarinet, marimba, piano, viola and cello; and also to display, though without any superficial showiness, the composer's own brilliant technique. For *Ave Maris Stella* is an example of real chamber music on a large scale rare for its time, eschewing the contrary colours and noisiness of *Antechrist* to concentrate on a sustained musical argument for a varied but cohesive sextet.

As the title implies, the work is based on the plainsong for the office hymn which praises the Virgin as 'star of the sea', a plainsong familiar from settings by Dunstable, Dufay, Monteverdi and others. No doubt Davies was influenced by these precedents in his choice, though he must also have been attracted by the text, of obvious relevance to a composer working over a wide bay in the long northern nights, and by the possibilities of the plainsong as a musical subject, to be explored with a far surer awareness of harmonic consequences than had been the case two decades before in his other Marian chamber piece, *Alma Redemptoris Mater.*

However, the presence of the plainsong is much less obvious here than in that earlier work, though there is no difficulty in detecting the use of what Davies points out is the work's other source, his own setting of a Greek text for his bookplate. Printed as a preface to the score, this has words which invite the reader, with a moral seriousness characteristic of Davies, to travel the path of wisdom and so combat philistinism. The same message was to be dramatized with a much lighter touch in his children's opera, *The Two Fiddlers.* Here the text is set as a monody in nine phrases, and this turns out to be a straightforward unfolding of a 'magic square' of pitches and durational values as follows:

C♯1	E♯6	B♯2	E 7	B 3	G♯8	A 4	F♯9	D 5
A 6	G♯2	B♯7	G 3	B 8	F♯4	D♯9	E 5	C♯1
D♯2	B 7	A♯3	D 8	A 4	C♯9	G♯5	E♯1	F♯6
G 7	E 3	C 8	B 4	D♯9	A♯5	D 1	A 6	F♯2
F×3	G♯8	E♯4	C♯9	B♯5	E 1	B 6	D♯2	A♯7
D♯8	B♯4	C♯9	A♯5	F♯1	E♯6	A 2	E 7	G♯3
A♯4	E♯9	C×5	D♯1	B♯6	G♯2	F×7	B 3	F♯8
D 9	F♯5	C♯1	A♯6	B 2	G♯7	E 3	D♯8	F×4
G♯5	D♯1	G 6	D 2	B 7	C 3	A 8	F 4	E 9

The grid of rhythmic values is readily obtained, starting from the 1 in the top left corner, adding five successively along the rows and down the columns while also subtracting nine whenever the total exceeds that figure. This produces a square in which the same sequence is repeated in rows and columns with progressive rotation, a square which is derived, as David Roberts has pointed out, from the numerologist's 'magic square of the moon' and so fitted for use in a work honouring the Virgin Mary in stellar guise.

The construction of the pitch square is more complex. Each row is a transposition of its predecessor with, again, rotation by one position but in the opposite direction with regard to the duration square. Thus, for example, the second row is a transposition of the first up a fifth, with the last member (D) becoming the first (A). As to the question of how this system relates to the *Ave Maris Stella* chant, Davies has said merely that the plainsong 'forms the backbone of the music . . . "projected" through the magic square of the Moon'; but it is worth noting that successive transpositions of the last member of the first row yield the sequence:

$$D—A—B—C—C\sharp—F\sharp–G\sharp —E—F$$

which has some connection with the opening of the Gregorian *Ave Maris Stella:*

$$D—A—B—G—A—B—D—C$$

Other features of the note square are also of interest. The rows exclude major seconds and tritones but are rich in thirds and fifths and, except where these are broken by rotation, each row includes consecutively the notes of two major triads: those of E and D in the case of the first, for instance. From this the whole work gains a leaning towards diatonic consonance, and yet there is also a contradictory element, for the nine-note mode of each row can also be regarded as the 'negative' of another major triad whose notes are excluded: that of D$\sharp$ in the case of the first.

All these rhythmic and pitch properties of the bookplate square are of importance in *Ave Maris Stella*, since the work is based very largely on journeys through it. This is specially apparent in the first section, an andante introduction, where the cello simply reads the square from left to right, top to bottom, to make a recitative of mounting intensity, joined later by the viola taking the same route backwards in 3 : 5 rhythmic proportions and the piano repeating the viola's path but moving six times as fast as the cello, while the alto flute chooses sequences more capriciously from the table in free rhythm and the marimba provides a slow harmonic support. The clarinet, absent from the opening section, has the principal voice in the second and undertakes another journey from the C at top left to the E at bottom right, but does so by reading along diagonals (C♯—A—E♯—D♯—G♯—B♯ etc.). Meanwhile here the flautist and the pianist choose different sequences from the square, branching out from the clarinet melody and back into it, criss-crossing each other and generally becoming more flamboyant as the pace inevitably quickens. For the different uses of the square in the cantus of these two sections leads, of course, to quite different rhythmic results: the cello line falls naturally into nine segments of equal length, with repetitions of particular groupings (perhaps most obvious is that consisting of the short value 1 between two values of similar, much longer duration), whereas the clarinet line proceeds in increasingly longer then shorter runs of equal values (1—6—6—2—2—2 etc.). It will also be apparent already how closely these 'magic square' procedures relate to the post-medieval techniques of Davies's earlier music: the cantus firmus as foundation, the mensural canons (Section 1) and the weaving of melodies into and out of the cantus (Section 2).

The following summary of the whole composition indicates the derivation of the principal line in each section:

1. Andante. Linear reading in cello from C♯ to E;
2. Poco a poco più moto. Diagonal reading in clarinet from C♯ to E;
3. Allegro. Spiral reading in marimba alternating with clarinet from central C (B♯) to top left C♯;
4. Prestissimo. Spiral reading in cello, viola and clarinet by turns from top left C♯ to central C (B♯);
5. Allegro. Various readings in canons between woodwinds and strings;
6. Moderato. Spiral reading in marimba solo from central C (B♯) to top left C♯;

7. Presto. Diagonal reading shared among ensemble in short fragments from C♯ to E;
8. Tempo del'inizio. Linear reading in flute, cello and clarinet by turns from C♯ to E;
9. Lento molto. Diagonal reading in marimba from E to C♯, followed by coda.

In terms of fundamental construction, therefore, and also in some points of instrumentation, there is an underlying palindromic arrangement, Section 1 corresponding with Section 8 (which is very clearly a repetition, though drastically modified, the original music being at first shot up two octaves, so that it is experienced not as a homecoming but more as a sudden re-opening of the argument), Section 2 with Section 7 (both winding up the music for a new turn of events, though in the second case with much greater tension) and Section 3 with Section 6 (both steady, serious developments). However, *Ave Maris Stella* is not by any means experienced as a symmetrically closed structure but rather as one which moves constantly onward, and this is due not only to the presence of a ninth section which breaks the palindrome but also, much more importantly, to Davies's long-range harmonic planning and his ability to create music which is powerfully propulsive both in surface gesture and in harmony.

The above précis of the work has already revealed the importance of C♯, C and E as goals, and here the properties of the 'magic square' fit in nicely with Davies's harmonic thinking in this work and many of its successors. For in the same way that the First Symphony has, according to the composer, 'tonics' and 'dominants' separated by a major third, so here the main poles may be seen as C♯ with a dominant of E♯ and C with a dominant of E: these four are the first pitches in the first row of the square, and they occur at other crucial points, directing the broad harmonic flow that has been outlined. And, though it would be quite wrong to describe *Ave Maris Stella* simply as being 'in C♯', it is not too misleading to regard it as being 'in flight from C♯'. Indeed, it would be entirely at one with Davies's musical personality that a tonal centre should

76

function not as a basis of rest and stability but as a spur to action.

This interpretation gains weight from the fact that the whole piece starts out from a C♯, that its heteroclite seventh section is sparked off by C♯s over a range of five octaves, and that the final lentissimo coda can be viewed as an attempt, successful as it turns out, to obliterate the C♯ that has been achieved with the harmonic process coming full circle. The entire ninth section is dominated by the dead cold sound of the marimba in even pulsations at a rate that changes seemingly haphazardly but is always slow, like drips from an icicle. It is an agonizingly protracted finale, as in some earlier works, but at last there come two confirmations of conclusion: the *Ave Maris Stella* plainsong is heard clearly for the first time, in the alto flute, though transposed up a fourth to fit into the harmonic ambience of the bottom row of the 'magic square', and the cello's first phrase comes back almost exactly reversed, but two octaves up in the clarinet (see Example 9, on p. 77).

There is yet, however, another page to follow, and here, with the utterly frozen violence of slow regular stabs, C♯ is effaced from the music and the ending, though equivocal, is in the region of C—E.

If the 'magic square' thus guides the melodic construction of *Ave Maris Stella*, its sectional structure (merely in respect of nineness) and its harmonic planning, it is also important to Davies's harmony on the smaller scale. For example, the marimba's chords in Section 1 are generally in thirds and sixths fastening on to elements in the cello's linear reading, and in Section 5 the piano announces the first row of the square reversed as a cantus harmonized with either the last six or the first three notes of the same row:

The registral placing of these chords, and their assignment to an instrument of inharmonic resonance, naturally suggests overtone structures, and indeed it might be possible to explain more general features of Davies's later harmony in terms of resonance phenomena. This would, of course, be all of a piece with the interest in bell sounds which has been mentioned, and which continues in the preference for tuned percussion shown not only in *Ave Maris Stella* but those works which would follow it, such as the First Symphony and *A Mirror of Whitening Light*.

Yet, though it is the marimba player who has the most exposed opportunities, in the cadenza that is Section 6 and also in the work's later stages, *Ave Maris Stella* admirably fulfils its purpose as a concerto for sextet and a masterpiece of compositional technique. Not only is it a feat of harmonic construction, it is also remarkable in achieving a complex six-part rhythmic polyphony that is practicable and fluid: Example 9 provides an instance of this. Its prevalent tone, however, is far from extrovert, for its ultimate and most extraordinary attainment is an intense luminosity that seems to be the reward of its intense inward concentration.

4 PAX ORCADIENSIS

Under this title Davies wrote an article in 1976 giving some hint of the feelings that have made Orkney not just a congenial but a necessary composing environment for him since his first visit in 1970. As he remarked in the article, there is 'no escape from yourself here, you just have to realize what you are through your music, with much more intensity than in urban surroundings'. And yet, of course, in his works of 1966–9 he had been very far from escaping: he had, rather, undertaken a creative self-examination at a depth approached by few composers since Schoenberg in his works of 1908–12. Orkney did not, therefore, throw him for the first time on to his own artistic resources, but rather it presented him with a physical environment which, as has been observed above, matched the interior landscape reached at the end of *Worldes Blis*. His arrival in Orkney was thus a psychological homecoming, and it enabled him to go straight into a new and extraordinarily prolific creative period without the long hiatus that Schoenberg needed in order to rediscover some grounds for composing. It also made it almost inevitable that a large proportion of his output since moving to Hoy should be directly stimulated by the Orcadian scene and culture.

At the same time, he might not so readily have discovered the Orkneyman within himself had he not had the guide of George Mackay Brown's poetry. In his article, he recalls the powerful impression Brown's work made on him when he encountered it during his first stay in Orkney, and it is significant that his first Orkney piece, apart from the score for *The Devils* (though even this contains what must be seen retrospectively as Orcadian atmosphere in its marimba-imbued slow meditations), was a setting of Brown's poem, *From Stone to Thorn*, for soprano, basset clarinet (the instrument in A with a specially low reach, developed by Alan Hacker for the Mozart concerto and used by Davies in several works), harpsichord, guitar and percussion (1971). This was the perfect bridge to a new expressive world because it allowed Davies to look again at an old one: the poem relates the Stations of the Cross to the seasons of the agricultural calendar, just as *Vesalii Icones* had related them to an anatomy lesson, only here the Stations are undisturbed from convention and the corresponding images are carved in a few words. It follows that the musical feeling is utterly different. Indeed, it is as if the first-person experience of the late Sixties has suddenly become third-person narration: hence the format of a concert piece for solo singer, hitherto an unknown genre in Davies's output. His earlier non-dramatic works with soloists—the Five Motets, the *Leopardi Fragments*, *Veni Sancte Spiritus* and *Ecce Manus Tradentis*—had all avoided extended writing for solo voices, either by using a duo or by restricting the soloists to very brief appearances, so that there is no danger of the singer coming to direct the musical expression: that could be permitted only when the singer was obliged to melt his personality into that of another, in *Revelation and Fall* and *Eight Songs for a Mad King*. *From Stone to Thorn* is, therefore, remarkably enough, Davies's first approximation to a song, or rather in this case to a solo cantata, and it was possible because he had for the first time discovered subject matter, in the Brown words and the harsh living conditions of Orkney they evoke, which he could interpret without irony.

Whether consciously or not, in setting the Brown text he nevertheless looked back to the nearest parallel among his earlier works, *Revelation and Fall*; for *From Stone to Thorn* is again a continuous developing structure forged upon a highly melismatic vocal line. The differences are that the new piece is quite objective in tone; that the short phrases of Brown's poem lead to shorter vocal arcs which keep coming to rest and completion instead of bounding forwards as they do in the Trakl piece; and, most obviously, that *From Stone to Thorn* is entirely a sung work, refusing the spoken, screamed and shouted utterances of its predecessor.

Relative decorum is also a feature of the accompaniment, which omits the two strings of the Fires formation and so excludes the opportunity for the kind of expressive intensity that had reached its climax in the cello solo of *Vesalii Icones*. There is no flute, though the clarinet is retained for a characteristically extravagant cadenza near the end of the work, even if that cadenza has in this work more the feeling of exultant virtuosity than, as in *Hymnos* for example, a desperate articulation of emotion. Most importantly, the timbral centre has now shifted to the area of plucked and struck sounds, with harpsichord and guitar joined by the percussionist's glockenspiel. Similar combinations of tuned percussion in polyphony had occurred quite often in Davies's music, as for instance in *Antechrist* or, to go back rather further, *Te Lucis Ante Terminum*, but never before had they determined the texture of a whole composition. Here they do, and the change in expressive effect is a marked one, for it is quite impossible that a harpsichord or a guitar should approach the potency of feeling that Davies could pack into wind or string lines. So by its instrumentation alone *From Stone to Thorn* is made cooler, more distant, and its innovations in this domain were to be followed in many succeeding scores.

The trend continued immediately in Davies's next work for the Fires, his *Hymn to St. Magnus* (1972), which was a first homage to the twelfth-century Orkney earl who was murdered at the behest of his cousin and soon revered as a martyr. Davies has said that the central parts of this four-movement work are 'permeated by the violence of the martyrdom and the violence of the sea', and so indeed they are, but the connection of a personal with an impersonal violence draws attention to the change taking place in his composing position at this time. Impassioned solos for viola and cello, flute and clarinet are still present in the massive third movement that is the work's gravitational centre, and yet the urgent force of the music comes more from the clash of overlapping structures in a complex interlocking of repetitions and variations, and also, on the surface level, from the perpetual activity of tuned percussion instruments—piano and marimba above all, as later in *Ave Maris Stella*, but also celesta, crotales and handbells. It is as if the resonances of these instruments, previously associated in a static manner with the ritual world of bells, had come gushing into life under the influence of the northern sea and light.

The mezzo-soprano voice in the *Hymn to St. Magnus* has retreated to assume an obbligato role. The soloist enters at the end of the short 'Introduzione' to chant a dedication, is absent from the following 'Sonata prima', enters sporadically in the second half of the 'Sonata seconda super "Sancte Magne"' with her sevenfold imprecation of 'Sancte Magne, ora pro nobis', and then finally comes to the forefront with Davies's setting of the St. Magnus hymn, *Nobilis, Humilis*. It is, of course, the original twelfth-century music for this hymn—Orkney's one earlier claim to a place in musical history, familiar to students as an example of the curious northern habit of writing organum in thirds instead of fourths or fifths—that forms the seed for the entire composition. It makes shadowy appearances in the first movement and again in the last, but its opening motif of a rising minor third followed by a falling minor second (an expression of the same motif that gave rise to *O Magnum Mysterium* and other works) can be felt to be the germinal influence on the grand development processes of the central sonatas.

If the second sonata, conceived as one massive urgent wave containing smaller flows of forward motion, relates most obviously to 'the violence of the sea', then 'the violence of the martyrdom' is perhaps most directly evoked in the first, whose climax is a passage of knife-like repeated notes in the woodwinds over strumming in the strings, which are to be held in the manner of ukulele and banjo, debased instruments which found a place that same year in the grotesque stage band for *Blind Man's Buff*. This barbaric music gives way on this occasion to an immense espressivo melody passing from cello to flute to clarinet to viola, a melody which in its intervallic construction, its slow tempo and its sustained trajectory of ascent and descent looks forward to the final setting of *Nobilis, Humilis*.

The second sonata is not distinctly sectioned like the first but geared to a constant presto tempo, which makes for a bewildering rapidity of development, despite the fact that the ear is guided by the insistent pitch repetitions that are prominent throughout. In its construction the movement is another essay in that favourite technique of superposing different musical structures, but this time paying explicit homage to the model in Monteverdi's 'Sonata Sopra Sancta Maria', not only in the title but also in having the soloist enter repeatedly, like the soprano chorus in the Monteverdi, with a prayer to the work's patron saint. These vocal phrases, in which the element of repetition is abundantly clear, draw attention to a basic principle of altered repetition in the instrumental music, for the first entry of the cello outside the running metrical framework (also the first of several such soft overlays on the music's strict backbone, these later including the vocal interjections), for instance, uses the flute-clarinet music from the start of the movement, though with staccato repetitions changed to smooth phrasing in a very typical inversion of musical effect.

Thus the *Hymn to St. Magnus* shows Davies's continuing absorption in early music, not just to the extent of taking up a local relic but also, more deeply, to that of discovering in pre-classical music ideas for the building of the most complex musical forms. It was, of course, unlikely that a mere change of locale or even style would alter so basic a facet of his musical personality, but it might not have been expected that on Hoy he would become more rather than less concerned with looking at music of the more distant past. Even the fact that he had to produce a repertory for the Fires does not sufficiently explain the stream of arrangements and reconsiderations, including works based on Buxtehude's cantata, *Also hat Gott die*

84

Welt geliebet (1971), on Gesualdo's responses for Tenebrae (1972), on Dunstable's motet, *Veni Sancte Spiritus* (1972), on two prelude-fugue pairs from Bach's *Well-Tempered Clavier* (1972–4), on Purcell's Fantasia on One Note (1973) and on sundry Scottish sacred pieces from the sixteenth century (1973–7) as well as a group of dances from the same source (1973). Some of these, like the Bach pieces, are straightforward instrumentations, though with quirks of colour that mark them distinctively as Davies's. For example, the prominent marimba in these Bach arrangements, coupled with the tonality of C♯, brings them near to *Ave Maris Stella*—and it is noteworthy that the Purcell fantasia shares, through transposition, the same tonal obsession. More generally, there is a favouring of those pitched percussion sonorities in pattering counterpoint that are so much a part of Davies's Orkney orchestration.

Very often, too, he imposes his own personality more forcefully and uses the original as a springboard for further endeavour, very much as he had done in the Seven In Nomine, not with the spike of parody that had entered into *Antechrist* and the earlier Purcell realizations. *Psalm 124* (1974), for instance, has three short movements for the Fires sextet (also available for organ as Three Voluntaries, 1976), each based on a Scottish original and each growing out from the renaissance material, the three being linked by little guitar interludes. In other works there is a clear separation between the old and the new: the Dunstable item is a straight instrumentation of his isorhythmic motet, but it is given a companion piece in a newly composed *Veni Creator Spiritus*, written for the same combination and alluding in its more spidery progress to the same basic ideas. Similarly, but with a much more dramatic effect, the secure faith of the Buxtehude cantata is suddenly undermined by a new instrumental interlude thrust between its movements. And in *Tenebrae super Gesualdo* the situation is similar but reversed, with the original music divided into short passages and arranged for soprano and guitar, to be enlarged upon in the interleaving new pieces for instrumental sextet.

Just as the Bach and Purcell pieces may be seen, with the benefit of hindsight, as studies in C♯ preparatory to *Ave Maris*

Stella, so the Gesualdo arrangement was followed by a pair of totally independent songs for voice and guitar, *Dark Angels* (1973), for which Davies once more turned to the poetry of George Mackay Brown. By comparison with *From Stone to Thorn* the vocal writing is drastically simplified, for not only is it largely syllabic, it is also much more straightforward in harmony and rhythm, the two songs, which are separated by a guitar solo, being rooted in symmetrical, repetitive structures. There is, indeed, something of the fresh melancholy of so much Scottish folk music in this very attractive little work, which is a lament for the tragedy of Rackwick, overshadowed by the 'dark angels' of its guardian hills. It is in the first song, 'The Drowning Brothers', that this tone of simple objective compassion is strongest, and particularly in its slow narrative chants, oscillating over a minor third, which set the scene for the tale of how the community lost its last two children in the burn and so withdrew to leave the 'Dead Fires' of deserted dwellings that are the subject of the more passionate second song.

Before 1970 Davies had used somebody else's words only in the *Leopardi Fragments*, *Revelation and Fall* and *Eight Songs for a Mad King*, preferring to set sacred texts or act as his own librettist. Now, however, within the space of two years he had twice taken poems by George Mackay Brown, and he was to do so with continued frequency in song cycles, choral works and operas, besides using quotations from Brown's poetry as titles for instrumental works: *The Seven Brightnesses* for clarinet (1975), for instance, draws a phrase from 'The Drowning Brothers'. Indeed, Davies in his Orkney period has used Brown's words almost to the exclusion of all other, the main exception being his second Randolph Stow collaboration, *Miss Donnithorne's Maggot*. Rather as in the case of Webern and Hildegard Jone, the composer found in the poet a sympathetic voice at a time of stylistic change, and the new manner became, in its vocal aspect, inseparably bound up with that poet's world. Yet this could not have happened unless, as in *From Stone to Thorn*, that world had not already overlapped with Davies's own.

86

The deep connection becomes increasingly apparent in his next two Brown settings, *Fiddlers at the Wedding* (1973–4) and *The Blind Fiddler* (1975), both of which expand the *Dark Angels* form of songs with instrumental interludes: there are seven movements in *Fiddlers* and fourteen in *The Blind Fiddler*. Both the later works also grow out of *Dark Angels* in their colouring, the first being for voice with alto flute, mandolin, guitar and percussion, the second for voice with the Fires sextet and guitar. (At this period the guitar was almost a standard of Davies's chamber instrumentation, appearing as it does in several of the Scottish recompositions, in the Septet created in 1972 from the Sextet of 1958, and in the opera, *The Martyrdom of St. Magnus*). In all three Brown song cycles the guitar obviously heightens the echoes of folksong, but its evanescent sonorities also suited Davies's purpose exactly in works that depend very much on harmonies glimpsed but not apprehended, and that concern themselves with the clear light and air of the cold north.

Like *From Stone to Thorn* and *Dark Angels*, *Fiddlers at the Wedding* takes its texts from Brown's collection, *Fishermen with Ploughs*, which is centred on the history and atmosphere of Rackwick. Of the four short poems, the first gives the cycle its rather misleading title, since the work is more about the life of the tinker than fiddlers or weddings, and also provides musical material for the three interludes, which appear as ever vaguer ripples from the opening. The whole work continues the simple manner of *Dark Angels*, with a marked feeling for G and Eb as tonal centres, and with the voice similarly intoning over light instrumental support.

The Blind Fiddler is the culmination of these Brown cycles and also of other trends in Davies's music during the first half of the Seventies. Its vocal writing partakes of the same cool lyricism that flows through *Dark Angels* and *Fiddlers at the Wedding*, but the third song also looks back to *Stone Litany* for mezzo-soprano and orchestra (1973) in decorating a declamatory line with quick, fractured ornaments. *The Blind Fiddler* was also the next major work to take up the harmonic methods of *Ave Maris Stella*. Again the progressions are related to a number square, but in this case a much simpler one, with seven-by-seven integers and a top row consisting simply of an ordering of the white-note mode. Fourths and fifths are important in the harmony, and, even more than in *Ave Maris Stella* or *Fiddlers at the Wedding*, there is a strong pull towards the focal pitches: B, C and G.

On another level *The Blind Fiddler* surveys, from its position of detachment, the music-theatre works of the previous decade, for it is an internal drama, the central character personified in the solo violin part and the singer now cast in the role of narrator. It is also, furthermore, yet another parallel to the Stations of the Cross, not only in having fourteen numbers but also in such specific correspondences as the concern of the sixth song with the death of the fiddler (already identified with Christ by the first song), or the ensuing placing of the violin in the maternal arms of the cello, or its final resurrection, rising from the singer's resting place of C to a high harmonic G♭, an exquisite but piercing negation.

However, *The Blind Fiddler* is not actively engaged in the questioning of religious truth in the manner of *Vesalii Icones*, for its central point, announced in the chorale-like second song, is that 'the lesser word, the fiddle, the poem, the rune, must work the miracle of bread', that spiritual and intellectual nourishment must be provided by art in a time when religion is a sealed book. The significance of this number is underlined by the echoes from it that arrive later in the cycle, notably in the third song, rather as the chorale-canon in *Revelation and Fall* is subsequently recalled. And, like that work, *The Blind Fiddler* is a powerfully integrated structure, with scherzo-like fiddle episodes in a distorted folk style (Nos. 3, 5, 7 and 11) to punctuate a work that proceeds as surely as *Ave Maris Stella* from an expository opening through a hard-driven, fragmented climax (here placed earlier, as No. 6) to a long slow dissolution.

After the group of works that had led up to *The Blind Fiddler* Davies abandoned the song format again, except for a late echo of the same world in *Anakreontika* for mezzo-soprano and quartet (1976) which, however, uses ancient Greek texts while sharing the alternating song–interlude form and the timbral atmosphere of the Brown cycles. The experience in word setting that he had gained would be put to use in the following rapid succession of theatre works, *The Martyrdom of St. Magnus* (1976), *Le Jongleur de Notre Dame* (1978), *The Lighthouse* (1979) and the two children's operas; meanwhile *Ave Maris Stella* and *The Blind Fiddler* had provided him with the harmonic and structural means that made possible the First Symphony (see note, p. 157).

The announcement of this work caused some surprise, even though the symphonic qualities of the Second Taverner Fantasia and *Worldes Blis* had long been recognized, for in the mid-Seventies it still seemed very odd that an 'advanced' composer should take up the most orthodox of musical forms. And indeed, as Davies's own account of the work's genesis reveals, it took him some time to realize that it was a symphony that he was writing. Though the score is dated 1975–6, the work was begun in 1973, the year of his first Orkney orchestral score: this was *Stone Litany* with mezzo-soprano obbligato (see note, p. 157), a single movement which, drawing powerfully argued orchestral developments from the material of an exotic world (in this case that of the runic incantations), suggests comparison with *St. Thomas Wake*. But where in that work the band's foxtrots were all grotesques, in *Stone Litany* the vocal interjections are each quite different in style and colour, and coolly laid out without irony. In the passage describing 'Ingibjorg, the fair widow', for instance, there is a sensuousness much more relaxed than anything in the *Leopardi Fragments*, contrasting starkly with the next inscription, where, with his agitated vocal virtuosity and his knife-like attacks in brass and percussion, Davies would seem to see 'Lif, the Earl's cook' as the butcher of St. Magnus in his future opera and 'Hakon' as the same work's evil commandant. But if the litany has its stones crying for vengeance, it is more generally a work evoking the ancientness, the wind, the flatness and the leaden light of the Maeshowe site, even with directly picturesque effects like the microtonal wind glissandos of the opening section.

The sound world here looks forward to the third movement

of the symphony, which as a whole follows *Stone Litany* in giving the tuned percussion a prominent place in the musical development. Indeed it goes further, for now there are no noise instruments, and the ensemble of harp, celesta, marimba, tubular bells, glockenspiel and crotales, though obviously useful in conveying the glinting light of a seascape, is employed much more importantly to carry quite as much musical weight as any other section of the orchestra, the marimba often repeating its central role in *Ave Maris Stella*. And there are further connections with that work in the pitch materials of the symphony, which sometimes uses the same 'magic square' and often employs similar, though more complex techniques to point and direct the main harmonic flow. Moreover, the plainsong *Ave Maris Stella* is one of the fundamental ideas at issue in the work's crucible of transformation.

What is most new about the symphony, of course, is its title, which is a statement not so much about the contents as about the way in which it is to be heard: that is, with expectations arising from the great symphonic literature from Haydn to Mahler and Sibelius. Thus after the big opening movement, with its pressing dynamism assured by the long single-note crescendos to which Davies's note refers (without mentioning that they go back in his orchestral output as far as *Prolation*), one is prepared for a slow movement, which the second movement at first appears to be. But then this music scampers off and evaporates as a presto, so that the need for an expansive centre is still more keenly felt by the time the adagio arrives, and yet at the same time this 'real' slow movement gains tension from one's fear that it may similarly turn into something utterly different. And within movements, too, Davies plays, as so often in the past, with frictions between expected and actual forms. Most obviously, the returns of the initial material in the outer movements are enough to sketch in the outlines of sonata structures, with repeated expositions, developments and recapitulations, but in fact the forms of these movements are a good deal more complex, switching from one clearly marked phase of development to another, these phases being at once parallel, in that they go over the same ground, and successive, in that they do so in very different terms to generate a continuously evolving structure. Furthermore, the fact that long melodic lines are rare in the symphony until the gathering unison string melody near the end makes it appear that this material, read from the *Ave Maris Stella* square transposed by a tritone, is the 'theme' towards which the whole work has been travelling, as in the case of *Worldes Blis*, and the highly inconclusive ending can be understood as a sign that the music has only now reached a state at which a real 'work' could begin.

Davies's comment that the symphony 'could mark the possibility of the beginning of an orchestral competence' draws attention to the preparatory nature of the piece, though it is also a remark of characteristic modesty that quite ignores the achievement of the Second Taverner Fantasia, *Worldes Blis*, St. *Thomas Wake* and *Stone Litany*, all powerfully argued and adroitly orchestrated works. These are certainly not juvenilia, even if, since the première of the First Symphony in 1978, they have gained a special nuance, like Brahms' St. Antoni Variations, as the winding-up essays of a symphonist. However, and this despite Davies's own disclaimer about there being 'no "orchestration" as such' in the work, the First Symphony does show a new degree of confidence and distinctiveness in the handling of orchestral sound, even by comparison with the very deft and poetic *Stone Litany*. Not only is the slow movement an effective sound picture of the weird, unpeopled Orkney landscape, but the tuned percussion constantly recalls the nearness of the sea, while on a more purely musical level, the junction of quite differently scored sections in the first movement is done with a careful ear for the balancing of textures to preserve a continuous onward thrust of invention.

It was hardly surprising that this breakthrough should have led quickly to other orchestral endeavours, not only to a Second Symphony (1980) but also to a single-movement piece for chamber orchestra, *A Mirror of Whitening Light* (1976–7, see note, p. 163) and a full-length ballet, *Salome* (1978, see note, p. 165). *A Mirror* is scored for a condensation of the First

Symphony's orchestra, and in its title it alludes to alchemical transformation as a metaphor which applies as much to the symphony's workings as to its own. It is also one of Davies's most beautiful works and, in its use of the 'key' of C with F and G as dominants, one of his easiest to follow, especially in its early stages, where C is repeatedly reinforced as focus and then the *Veni Sancte Spiritus* plainsong grows into 'magic square' patterns in the manner of *Ave Maris Stella*.

In *Salome* the chant is very much nearer the surface. Often the chosen plainsong melodies are presented without the usual transposition, even if to un-vocal rhythmic patterns, and the result is a piece whose feeling of modality is very much more definite than is at all usual in Davies's music for professionals. Clear modality is, of course, a natural technique for a work set in the ancient east, and the infection of palpably modal melodies with dissonant harmonies and extraordinary instrumental effects contributes much to an evocation of corrupt power and of sexual mixed with religious hysteria, this in a manner more objective than Davies had wanted to achieve in *The Devils* and, by the way, owing nothing to Strauss's opera. Davies is equally independent in the striking pictorial impressions he manages to create through the use of an orchestra in which tuned percussion is again prominent, though joined once more by a wide spectrum of noise instruments. The baptism scene (Act I, Scene IV) has rippling music for percussion and strings anchored to a slow, quiet wind polyphony, an image of water which is created entirely within Davies's own style and yet perfectly descriptive. Again, the demands of writing a big ballet score, which had of necessity to include a variety of rhythmic styles, leads Davies at some points to emulate the sprightly metrical shifts of Stravinsky and so create music which is rather different from anything he had done before but is nevertheless wholly his own. And, bearing in mind that Stravinsky's own ballets were all one-acters, *Salome* must be counted among the few great full-length ballet scores since *The Sleeping Beauty*.

While Davies was extending his international reputation through these orchestral works, he was far from neglecting his own immediate locality, for it was there that in 1977 he founded the St. Magnus Festival, based on the cathedral raised in honour of Orkney's patron saint at Kirkwall. Fittingly, the first festival opened with a new opera by Davies on the subject of the saint's life and death, *The Martyrdom of St. Magnus* (see note, p. 162), performed within his own cathedral. However, a note in the score indicates that the work is intended preferably for performance in the round, helping to make it clear to the audience that, rather as in Britten's church operas, they are witnessing the enactment of a parable. For *Magnus* is a much more objective piece than *Taverner*. The small orchestra, consisting of the Fires sextet with added guitar and brass trio, does not weave the central character's flow of thought but instead provides him with a musical environment, an environment appropriately rooted in plainsong—and this too, of course, suggests a parallel with the Britten parables.

Davies prepared his own text for the opera after George Mackay Brown's novel, *Magnus*, which takes the story of the saint as a fable of the individual sacrificed to assuage bestial instinct and blind ideology; in both book and opera the perpetual relevance of the tale is pointed by a final updating to a time much nearer the present. Much of the action, however, is situated firmly in the twelfth century, where Magnus is seen first at the Battle of Menai Strait, seated in a longship reciting a psalm while Vikings and Welshmen wage war with words and arrows. Boasting a pair of trumpets to lead the fanfares, a horn to whoop through two octaves in a virtuoso image of animal power for the King of Norway, and racing tuned percussion in the heat of the battle, this opening scene sets the tone of emblematic presentation. Further enhancement of the objective tone comes from the presence of a chorus figure in Blind Mary, who introduces the action in a long solo accompanied only by guitar, and who appears again to put her curse on the rival earls, Magnus and Hakon, in the third scene and once more at the end to drive home the message of the opera. At the same time her vocal line, reminiscent of the Brown song cycles, prepares one for a style much simpler and freer than that of *Taverner*.

Yet the parallels between the two operas persist. Magnus's tragedy, like Taverner's, is sealed in a temptation scene (Scene II) and, though from this Magnus emerges not as persecutor but as destined victim, his fate has been determined just as inexorably. In the fourth scene the Bishop expresses the redemptive need for a martyr, but Magnus has already sensed this, and the whole second half of the opera is concerned with an inevitable road to death, leading Magnus first by sea to the island of Egilsay in a scene illuminated with musical pictures of sea waves and a rowed boat. Then, with the first appearance of Hakon, refusing any compromise (Scene VI), Davies begins to recapture the frightening ferocity of his earlier works of music theatre, opening in Scene VII into a brilliant sequence of pastiches that musically bring the time forward from the twelfth century to the twentieth, eventually arriving, it comes as no surprise, at a foxtrot.

The final horror comes with Hakon, now an anonymous military officer, shrieking and cajoling as he orders his butcher, Lifolf, to undertake the murder, which he duly does after Magnus, now simply 'the prisoner', has eloquently sung of the need for sacrifice to cleanse 'the mystery of evil'. After this, in Scene IX, the martyrdom is proved to have been an acceptable sacrifice, for Blind Mary receives her sight and Magnus, in the litany of chanting monks, takes his place among the northern saints. However, the opera ends not in triumph but with accusation, as Mary demands of the audience how long the cycle of sacrifice must continue. And thus, although *The Martyrdom of St. Magnus* is an Orkney piece created for an Orkney occasion, it is very firmly universalized.

Davies's subsequent works for his own festival have been no less successful in marrying local interest with general worth. They include two children's operas, *The Two Fiddlers* for secondary school resources (1978) and *Cinderella* for younger children (1979–80, see note, p. 169), of which the former is based on a George Mackay Brown story and the latter adds Orkney reference to the familiar fairy tale, though in neither case have parochial features stood in the way of wider acceptance, for both pieces are so sure in their aim, so unpretentious yet also so unpatronizing, that in the field of 'educational' music they are quite outstanding. And though the immediate stimulus may have come from the wish to include Orkney people directly in their own festival, the two operas came at a time when Davies's thoughts were returning to music for children, as witness the little piano book, *Stevie's Ferry to Hoy* (1977), written for a neighbour's daughter, the Three Studies (1975) for percussion orchestra, the children's band in *Le Jongleur de Notre Dame* and the *Kirkwall Shopping Songs* (1979) created specially for Kirkwall primary children.

The Two Fiddlers might be expected from its title to have some links with the earlier song cycles, and indeed it does contain dances for solo violin that in their folky but thoroughly individual modal style stand with the dance interludes from *The Blind Fiddler* and the 'Square Dance' for unaccompanied violin that rather curiously opens *Salome*. Yet this sternly moral piece is concerned less with the power of music than with the virtue of work. Storm Kolson, one of the two fiddlers, is waylaid by the trolls and obliged to play for them, in return for which they grant his wish that men will no longer have to work. While Storm imagines he is detained only a day, in fact twenty-one years have passed in the human world, and his friend, Gavin, has become the proud possessor of wife and family, car and bungalow, whiskers and walking stick, all achieved in a brisk parody of middle-class materialism. Meanwhile the people, freed from toil, have become fat and lethargic, spending their time in watching television or listening to records. Storm is distressed: this decline into passivity is not at all what he had intended. He breaks the spell with a new fiddle solo, and the opera ends with a warning against the deadening effect of mental laziness and pap entertainment. On a very simple level, therefore, this little opera manifests that view of art implicit in all Davies's output: that a work is not to be meekly accepted but actively understood, and that one of the most valuable things an artist can do is cause his audience to think.

Of course, besides being high-minded, *The Two Fiddlers* was made to be fun to perform, and the same live practicality informs Davies's major work for the following festival, *Solstice of Light* (1979), a cantata for tenor, chorus and organ designed for the amateur St. Magnus Singers. This was his second choral setting of a Brown text, preceded by *Westerlings* for unaccompanied voices (1976–7), which belongs more to the professional repertory, with its powerful vocalized seascapes to separate the songs of Norsemen colonizing Orkney, though it does end with a setting of the Lord's Prayer in the old Orcadian language of Norn that looks back to the simple and sombre manner of *O Magnum Mysterium*.

That precedent is still more directly evoked, and continuously, by *Solstice of Light*, which has, once again, fourteen numbers, though this time without any reference to the Stations of the Cross. Instead the work is a miniature poetic history of Orkney, beginning with its emergence from under 'the gray hands of ice', continuing with descriptions of the coming waves of settlers, prehistoric, Celt and Norse, and ending with a prayer to St. Magnus which is also a prayer that the islands' newfound mineral wealth shall not disturb the peace of the Orkney people nor that of the world. The five movements for organ solo inevitably recall the concluding fantasia of *O Magnum Mysterium*, if only because the organ is rather rare in Davies's music; in style the pieces are much more brilliant and varied in imagery, ranging from the almost unbearably slow build-up of 'Invocation of the Dove' to the athletic vigour of 'Earth Breakers, Hewers of Mighty Stone'. There is another departure from the earlier carol sequence in the closer liaison between the choral songs and the organ interludes: not only is the organ now often drawn into an accompanying role, but also the interludes themselves, though more daring than the songs in rhythm and harmony, lead out of and back into the choral world with no great wrench. As for the songs, they are often very close to the carols of *O Magnum Mysterium* in their stark modality laden with sevenths and tritones, though the main tonal centre is now C, often with a prominent E♭ that gives a suggestion of the minor mode.

The commitment to contemporary Orkney issues displayed in the final prayer of *Solstice of Light* was continued in *Black Pentecost* for mezzo-soprano, baritone and orchestra (1979) and

Claus Ørsted

Fleming Flindt and Vivi Flindt in *Salome*

Alex 'Tug' Wilson

Michael Rippon, David Wilson-Johnson and Neil Mackie in *The Lighthouse*

Gunnie Moberg

A scene from *Cinderella*

also, on a lighter but more cutting level, in the set of cabaret songs *The Yellow Cake Revue* (1980), devised as a St. Magnus Festival entertainment. Using the title that the First Symphony had a few years before outgrown, *Black Pentecost* is itself something of a symphony, with four movements playing continuously, though at the same time it is also a dramatic cantata, a fierce, powerful and at times bitterly ironic denunciation of the inhumanity of big industrial enterprise. That Davies could create such a protest entirely on his own terms is some measure of the strength of his technique and the flexibility of his now totally individual style, allowing him to compose almost simultaneously a Second Symphony and an opera for young children, a group of cabaret songs and a ghost story, *The Lighthouse* (see note, p. 167), where corrupted tonality is used to very different but equally effective purposes in driving home the destructive beastliness that lies so near below the surface of civilized man.

All the evidence of Davies's mastery is contained in the symphony itself. Although the orchestra is almost exactly the same as that which he had used in his First Symphony, and although the music is again coloured by the sounds of Orkney, the Second Symphony is very much clearer than its predecessor, both in form and in harmonic process. Its themes are more strongly underlined on the surface of the music, often by means of an obvious opposition between adjacent ideas: an unmistakable instance of this occurs right at the beginning of the work, as Davies has pointed out (see note, p. 171), where after a brief introduction, arrested rather than slow, the first movement starts with ripping horn chorales answered by strenuous melodies in the violins. It is tempting to regard this whole section as an exposition, which is perhaps recapitulated later in the movement when there is a no less definite question-answer routine for groups of trumpets and of trombones.

Also characteristic of the Second Symphony, particularly of the first and last movements, is an almost Varèsian sense of the drama of orchestral sound. Here Davies's acknowledged influence of the sea may be misleading if it suggests something along the lines of *La Mer*, for the symphony's atmosphere is much more one of turmoil, of great waves of sound landing with a crash, of surging volumes channelled through narrow openings, of fierce reflections that make the water too brilliant to behold (one thinks again of *A Mirror of Whitening Light*). The excited cascades of woodwind arpeggios, which have been a feature of Davies's orchestral world since the First Taverner Fantasia, return to mark climactic moments, but there are many similarly impressive things that are quite new, like the ending of the second movement, with a trumpet melody thrust up through a massive orchestral crescendo.

The willingness to encompass such striking details of scoring has evidently stayed with Davies since *Salome*, which is more remarkably recalled by the extraordinary near-tonal writing of parts of the finale and much of the third movement, as well as by dance-like passages bound to constant rhythmic figures: the alarming invasion of bouncing iambs in the first movement, or the almost perpetual semiquaver rush of the scherzo. This latter movement seems much the most direct of the four, and yet its tonality, utterly characteristic of Davies and looking back as far as *O Magnum Mysterium*, is already opening the way to a converge between the most straightforward and the most complex kinds of harmony.

Quite apart from its inherent merits, Davies's Second Symphony is bound to excite intense interest merely by its existence, for not since the Thirties has a composer of the front rank embarked on a series of works in the most challenging and public of forms. One must wait and watch as Davies goes on his way, though it is impossible to refrain from conjectures about the sounds and shapes of his Third Symphony, his Fifth, his Ninth.

Part Two

Conversations with the Composer

The following is a transcript of conversations in London on 1 February and 21 May 1980, between which dates Davies was on Hoy composing the first movement of his Second Symphony.

Question: *I read somewhere that one of the earliest formative influences on you was being taken to 'The Gondoliers' when you were four. Did you start to compose straight after that?*

Davies: No. But I know what I did do: I made up tunes and sang them to myself. What they were like I've no idea, but I remember the event of composing them in my head and considering whether they should go up or down. I had no idea of notation.

You weren't playing the piano?

No. But going back to *The Gondoliers*, the music itself appealed very strongly, and the whole idea of creating on stage this bright glittering world—well, that appealed to the child very much. It was very different from the working-class background I was brought up in. And I realized even at that stage that this was something that possibly presented an alternative to working, for instance, either in my grandfather's shop or in a factory, which made a lot of noise, which I hated.

When did you get to learn notation?

When I was eight and was sent for piano lessons. The family piano wasn't being used—it was in my grandmother's house—and I was asked if I would like to play the piano. I said yes, and so it was moved to our house, and I was sent for lessons and learned to read notation.

And to write?

Immediately I wrote, yes. Very simple things: I was learning out of Smallwood's tutor books.

Was school music important?

No, not at all. At grammar school there was a very nice lady called Miss Clough who came and taught classes of ninety children once a week, but what can you do? Just sing. And then when it came to 'O'-level I asked the headmaster if I could do music, and he said: 'No, this is not a girl's school.' So when it came to 'A'-level I didn't tell him; I just did it. And then when I got a Lancashire County music scholarship on the result of that, he claimed credit for the school. It was a great insight into human nature.

How did you prepare for that 'A'-level exam?

I just did it. It's very elementary stuff. I remember going for the oral examination at Manchester High School for Girls: Annie Warburton was the examiner. One of the set works was the Beethoven fiddle concerto, and in the prospectus it said you had to be prepared to answer questions on this. Of course, I could play the whole thing on the piano, and that seemed to amaze this lady. She asked me what other works by Beethoven I could play without the score, so I said, 'You name it.' So she said, 'Symphony No. 1,' and I played a bit of that, 'Symphony No. 2,' and I played a bit of that, and we went right up to No. 9. That was more or less the end of the examination.

How were your musical tastes developing at this time? Apart from Beethoven.

Well, you see, in Manchester there was one great advantage, and that was the Henry Watson Music Library, which I more or less rifled. I think I knew every damned score they had in that place that was serious: just by playing them through on the piano you learn an awful lot. But, of course, there was absolutely nobody whom I could discuss these things with, and so it was all bottled up and very unformed, and it couldn't really surface in many ways until I was at the university and college in Manchester, where I met Birtwistle and Goehr and Ogdon and so on.

Was there any medieval or renaissance music among all those scores you were taking home?

There was the *Tudor Church Music* collection.

Did that have any influence on what you were writing?

Not at that stage. It was probably during my first year at university, in 1953, that I really got stuck into that, and then I suppose it only began to show around 1955–6.

Which was the period of your first published works: the Trumpet Sonata and the op.2 piano pieces. Do you still feel those pieces are your work?

Oh yes, very much. I can hear my own voice there all right.

In what things?

Ways of construction—already in the piano pieces there are isometric designs—and the harmony I can hear to be still the same kind of language that's coming out now. I think that ultimately that's something that no matter how you organize your music you've got no control over. There are archetypes somewhere in the mind, and they just come out and out and out.

How did you come to use early music at that time? It wasn't at all an obvious thing to do.

I don't know. I remember we discussed it in Manchester, but the others in that little circle were not interested—Birtwistle to some extent, but he didn't do it then. I was accused of burying my head in the sand so that I wouldn't have to face the questions of how to write music now. But I didn't see it like that at all: I just wanted to learn what I could from those composers and from plainsong. I could see in it so many pointers to large-scale design and, though I didn't then realize how it would work, there was some kind of instinctive complete sense of the rightness of it.

What about the impact of contemporary music?

When I was fourteen or fifteen Bartók, Schoenberg and Stravinsky were the really important people. Later on Messiaen became very important, and then in those very early years at university occasionally you'd hear or be able to get hold of a score of something like Boulez's Second Piano Sonata, or some of those early Nono things, or Stockhausen's *Kontra-Punkte*. Those pieces triggered something off: they were very liberating.

Who was teaching you composition?

Nobody. I started at the university music department as a composer student, but after two or three lessons I was slung out, which suited me, because I quickly realised that I would find no stimulation and no interest in doing the kinds of things they required their composer students to do, and that you'd be much happier, if you had any sense at all, finding out things for yourself.

ROME—CIRENCESTER—PRINCETON

Then in 1957 you took the decision to go and study with Petrassi in Rome. Why not with Messiaen?

I wanted to go to Italy. Also, Petrassi was prepared to give me more time and individual attention, whereas with Messiaen it was a question of going to a class.

Did you gain a lot from the experience?

Yes. Petrassi was very clever. He took a great deal of trouble looking at my scores and my sketches, and he'd ask questions. The lesson consisted basically of questions, and I had to

104

answer sensibly and carefully. If there was something wrong with my answer he would really interrogate me.

Then when you came back from Italy you took a job teaching at Cirencester Grammar School, and composing things like 'O Magnum Mysterium' and the 'Five Klee Pictures'. How were those pieces received by the children and your colleagues?

The kids came to terms with it very quickly. Members of staff: that was more difficult. A lot of them thought they knew what music ought to be, and this wasn't what it sounded like. I'm afraid that kind of thing you learn to ride fairly roughshod over and state your own point of view quite noisily.

I got the kids improvising and composing a lot, and watching and listening to them I learned a lot, too. It de-inhibited me, if you like.

And there was a more specific effect in that performing the Monteverdi Vespers in Cirencester led to that work's influencing your own. What were the connections?

Generally structural things. The way that the 'Sonata Sopra Sancta Maria' is tied together—which is an old polyphonic thing, extended—with the cantus going over the double barline and just draping, and sections happening underneath that, block-fashion but not absolutely parallel with it, so that you have two forms working together: in the String Quartet that was particularly important. And then the opening movement of the Sinfonia, for instance, has got a very obvious relationship on a very crude level with the opening of the Vespers.

Were there any other works that you performed at Cirencester that had repercussions of this kind?

No, the Vespers was the one that sparked a lot off.

And then you went to Princeton to study with Sessions. Did you also, while you were there, learn anything from Babbitt?

He's got a very clear mind, and I think I did learn something from him. I found, though, that his language is very hard to penetrate. He's obsessed with arithmetic, and I'm not very good at that: I can hear arithmetic, but I can't add my change.

And while you were in Princeton you wrote the first act of 'Taverner'.

Yes, and the Second Taverner Fantasia. It was the first time I'd had the chance to sit down and write music all day and all night if I wanted to.

TAVERNER/MAGNUS

It seems rather odd that you should have gone to America and started work on an opera on an English subject, even though you'd been working on it since the mid-Fifties.

Yes, though I hadn't worked on it intensively. But in Princeton University Library they had all the material and, if they hadn't actually got it, they'd got it on microfilm. So there was no problem.

Do you see that opera as a metaphor of a personal creative situation, in the same way that one can read Schoenberg's 'Moses und Aron', say, though he denied it?

Quite honestly, I don't know. I suppose that there's a grain of truth in that, that I was projecting myself into Taverner, but I think it was bigger than me. It was the situation not only of the creative artist but of anybody who believed in anything, and who could have this belief corrupted so that it started to eat into him and destroy him. The historical Taverner was probably just a peg to hang the thing on: I don't know, because I don't know very much about him. But I love to do this, to take a figure who has got a touch of reality, or a situation which is based on reality, and then let fantasy work.

And I think we see parallels with Taverner all the time, with people who become party-liners and their humanity as such disappears. It doesn't matter whether they're political or religious figures: the two are very much the same, in that they can become equally fanatical, equally inhuman. Classic examples are people like Calvin, betraying his own family,

106

and the Quaker Fox, betraying his second in command when he really needed his help, and on the highest principles. But at the time when I wrote *Taverner* I was very much concerned with the figure of Shostakovich, whose music doesn't say what it appears to say on the surface. Those triumphant finales, like the one in the Fifth Symphony—they ring so hollow, and they make a political statement by inversion, if you like. He, I think, has many parallels with Taverner, in that he mounted statements which would make it appear that he was totally with the régime in Russia since 1917, but his music itself always made one wonder. The parallel with Taverner, of course, is only that the two were composers under pressure: their reactions were completely different. Taverner, as far as I know at the time of writing the opera, went along with the new régime completely and believed in it, and gave up his humanity to become an inquisitor.

You wrote your own text for 'Taverner'.

Yes, though even now I'm told so often that I shouldn't write my own texts, that this is dangerous, because look at the mess composers make of their work. Well, some don't. I'm quite prepared to stand by what I do, and if it's dangerous, then we live by danger. Of course, you are sticking your neck out—much more than in just writing music, because you're taking the whole responsibility. But it does become necessary when the images are so strong that nobody else could write them.

I remember doing the text of *Taverner* in Princeton, and it was presenting itself to my mind quite literally as pictorial images, particularly images to do with the Jester becoming the Death figure and controlling the whole operation. They were just flashing into my mind, and I had to put them down as quickly as I could catch them. I think a lot of it was coming out of some source which I can only recognize when it happens.

And were the musical images coming as well?

Yes, the basic images. Of course, one worked out the syntax and the grammar very carefully, but the musical images behind—if you can distinguish those from what comes on the page—were intuitive.

Were you working to a groundplan in 'Taverner' and the Second Fantasia? Did you know, for instance, that the Fantasia was going to be in thirteen sections?

No, I didn't. I made a groundplan which I remember changed as the music was happening: it took on different features. That often happens. The opera, of course, was very firmly established by the text, and it didn't change once I'd done that. It already had the sort of noise that I wanted it to have in my mind, obviously.

I've been struck recently by the connections between 'Taverner' and your second opera. 'The Martyrdom of St. Magnus'. On the simplest level, the two protagonists are both tenors, and there aren't many tenor parts in your music. Then they're both tempted by the sword, which Taverner accepts and Magnus rejects. And there are even little details, like Magnus's Tempter-Monk coming in singing the 'Gloria Tibi Trinitas' plainsong which is so important in 'Taverner'.

Yes, the same images were coming through; it was another discussion of the same thing. Perhaps I shall write the same opera nine times, just as Bruckner wrote the same symphony nine times.

Yet in style it's quite different. To me, 'Taverner' is a first-person opera, seen through the eyes of the main character, whereas 'Magnus' is a third-person opera.

Yes, it's much more distanced; the point of view has definitely shifted.

And the whole issue of betrayal is treated quite differently, isn't it? Magnus's betrayal is not very important as an event, but his sacrifice is very much seen as necessary and positive, whereas Taverner's conversion is negative.

Yes, I totally agree with you there. It's a discussion of a related figure, but done in a very different way, and any parallels I could I pointed with the same kind of musical imagery.

For instance, in the inquisition scene, with the concentration-camp chief or whatever he is, I was very conscious of parallels with the interrogation by the jester in *Taverner*. Lifolf I see as a projection of Magnus himself, the fulfilment of his destiny of having to be sacrificed, and Magnus knows that he's got to go: it's almost a thing that he's willed upon himself in order to make things go smoothly, which he has a premonition they will, and that something positive will come out of this. I was also thinking here of Thomas à Becket.

But Becket, in the Eliot play, saw that a willed sacrifice would be no good. Magnus's sacrifice is very much willed.

That's right, he contradicts himself: he's very human. I was certainly conscious that he was a weak human being, and occasionally that comes to the surface, like when he's tempted by marriage and he almost wills himself to see it in completely negative terms. There he's contradicting both the Keeper of the Loom and the Tempter: the two figures are each a parody of the other, and sometimes I think it's quite hard to know which is on whose side. Of course, that whole scene is very much a projection out of his mind: it's really a dialogue between himself and his conscience.

CRISIS

'Taverner' marked the end of a phase in your music, didn't it?

Yes, all those early works, up to about 1964, I think of as apprentice pieces. I knew what I was doing: I was building up a solid foundation of compositional technique, and the last two things I did like that were *Taverner* and the Second Taverner Fantasia.

Even as early as 1962 I could feel that there was something about to happen which was going to burst out of the style in which I was then writing, and you can already feel that in the Second Fantasia and in the opera. I wasn't aware what the musical consequences of the upheaval were going to be, but I knew that I had to have enough technique to be able to withstand the shock of it. And had I not been quite thorough

109

about very boring things like being able to work canons in lots of different ways, I wouldn't have been able to mould the expressionist material of a work like *Revelation and Fall* so that it made coherent and formal sense. Isorhythmic workings and canon on a modular system of transformations made that piece possible, which otherwise would have been very incoherent.

Did the upheaval have anything to do with Act I, Scene IV of 'Taverner', where you're working with spiritual and psychological material at a deeper level than ever before?

That's a part of it, I'm sure, that very scene: a first expression of it which then became—I'm talking about just the text now—the kernel out of which not only texts but musical ideas grew. It was one of the seminal events, the composition of first the text and then the music; it became very important to me. But the upheaval was a slow one, and by the time *Revelation and Fall* was composed it had already been happening for a few years. I was quite consciously preparing for that work in the music and the texts I was doing in 1962–3.

Then somebody gave me a book of Trakl's work, and I was so thrilled by it that I just sat up the whole of one night reading through it, and I sketched out the dramatic shape of *Revelation and Fall* there and then. It was as if I'd worked on it already; it was almost like writing down a piece I knew.

'Revelation and Fall', though it's for a big ensemble, was one of the first pieces you did with your own group, then called the Pierrot Players. Did you have any idea, when you were getting that group together, that you were going to go into music theatre?

Actually, Birtwistle did the work of getting the players together, because I was in Australia at the time. And he was the one who was keenest at that stage on writing music theatre. I didn't realize I was going to do that, though later I realized it was something I was going to enjoy doing very much.

Had you not thought of 'Revelation and Fall' as a theatre piece in the first place?

Yes, but only in a very limited way. I didn't realize what the implications were, that it was going to develop so much. I had no idea that the *Eight Songs for a Mad King*, for instance, were just around the corner, although even then I had got a fairly complete sketch for the text of the opera that I'll be writing fairly soon, *Resurrection*. As in the case of *Taverner*, it's something I haven't been able to do because until now I haven't had the technique, but after writing all those music-theatre works and so on I'll be able to do it.

'Eight Songs' was unusual among your theatre pieces in that you used a text by someone else.

Yes, that was Randolph Stow. I met him first in New York and then in Australia, and we had the idea of collaborating on something—poems set to music as a concert piece, or whatever. He came up with this idea of doing something on George III, and at first it wasn't going to be a music-theatre piece, but then I had this extraordinary idea of putting the players in cages and making the king interact with them. That was when the poems were already under way and I'd got the first two.

The other odd thing about *Eight Songs* was the idea of taking lots of different materials and putting them together. I've never gone in for a very simple montage of unrelated objects which, for instance, Berio has done. To me it's always been much more appealing to take something where you can actually sense the distortion process happening.

As in 'Missa Super l'Homme Armé'?

Yes. There again the material presented itself to my mind without my being in control of it. I was doodling, if you like, and the material I was working with, the original anonymous *L'Homme Armé* mass, was making me laugh by distorting itself into all sorts of funny musical images, and I wrote them down. It just seemed to be a very natural product of something that was in my mind anyway—an extension, I suppose, of the grotesqueries in *Revelation and Fall*. And there are also parallels in visual art: not only the gargoyles and so on in medieval art but also things like Ensor and Grosz and Bacon. It seemed to be part of the atmosphere of the time.

111

Does it worry you that people don't know how to react to works like 'Eight Songs' and 'L'Homme Armé', where something that starts out being serious suddenly turns, say, into a foxtrot?

I think this is something that people rather enjoy coming to terms with and thinking about. I don't think they object to that—all right, in the first instance they did object and found it all very disturbing.

But surely those works are still intensely disturbing, because if a work is, in effect, mocking parts of itself, then one has nothing that one can with certainty take seriously.

Yes, exactly, and that's the intention. When I say these pieces aren't disturbing any more, I just mean they don't any longer create the kind of silly superficial disturbance which gets in the way of actually understanding a piece. On a deep level I think the music still is disturbing, and I hope it will go on being so.

I remember at that stage having an obsession with masks: the jester's mask, for instance, in *Taverner*, where it's quite an important thing, particularly when it's removed. What's the mask? Is the thing underneath still a mask? Then there's *Blind Man's Buff*, which is one of the tightest expressions of this whole preoccupation with what is real and what is not real, what is meant and what is parody, and exactly what *is* parody.

I think of a parallel with Liszt's 'Faust Symphony', where the 'Mephisto' movement parodies, almost in your own vicious terms, what has gone before. But then he redeems the whole thing with this great closing chorus. There's never any redemption in your music: one's left really not knowing what to take seriously.

Absolutely. No comment!

VESALII ICONES

The last of that early clutch of music-theatre works was 'Vesalii Icones'. To what extent did you organize the dance for that?

I made suggestions, but the choreography was William Louther's. It was my idea to use the Vesalius images super-

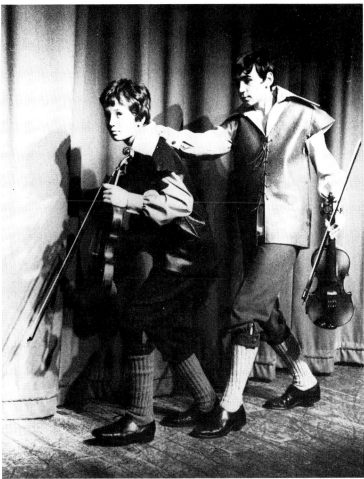

Gunnie Moberg/Boosey and Hawkes

Ian Tait (Storm) and Peter Marshall (Gavin) in *The Two Fiddlers*

Gunnie Moberg

Mark Furneaux (Brother Mark), Beverley Davison (Statue of the Virgin)
and David Campbell (Brother David) in *Le Jongleur de Notre-Dame*

imposed on the Stations of the Cross, with the little twist at the end, but the actual choreography was his, including, for instance, the idea in 'The Death of Christ', which I like very much, describing the spiral down to the still centre of that piece and then bursting out of it right at the end where it goes all Hollywood and ridiculous. And in the St. Veronica movement, where all the activity is inside the music, with all that network of cross-references going on and getting distorted, he just moves with an imaginary cloth and there's almost no activity—that was his idea.

He was getting it movement by movement. I was in Bristol at the time, coming to London to meet him and discuss it, then going back to write some more. It was a very quickly written piece.

Did you work in a similar way on 'Salome'?

That was also very much a collaboration, in that I spent a couple of days in the early stages in this hotel somewhere in the north of Denmark and just went through it with Flemming Flindt, scene by scene, texture by texture, length by length, discussing the dance, the mood. The whole thing was gone through very carefully, so that he felt as if he knew the music already before he'd heard a note of it. But the basic ideas in the scenario were his, not mine.

Going back to 'Vesalii Icones', that work seems to me an ending: it was the last work in which you concerned yourself very directly with spiritual matters in the surface of the music—

Yes, they go inside after that. 1969 was a critical year, and out of it came the music that I started to write in Orkney. I decided I didn't want to go on discussing these things and making these rather extravagant gestures. I wanted to take it much more inside the music.

Yes, the trouble with extravagant gestures is that they remain extravagant gestures. The ending of 'Vesalii Icones', the profane resurrection, is very shocking, but it's a unitary thing: one doesn't look for musical meaning at a deeper level. No doubt the foxtrot there is related to other things that have been going on in the music—

113

Sure.

—but one just accepts it as a foxtrot. It could almost be any foxtrot.

I don't know. I think it can only be that one, but then I'm prejudiced. But quite seriously, that sort of gesture is OK at that sort of stage in your career and that sort of age, but if you go on making it, it becomes tired, and there's just no point. I realized then that this had got to stop.

And what's much more interesting in that piece is the cello solo.

Oh yes. A lot of the writing for the group is there—even on the surface level, as in the movement where Christ takes the Cross—to set up around the cello an atmosphere which isolates it completely. In that case you have big city noises, even down to the traffic honking, which is very silly and very superficial, but which sets up this tremendous atmosphere, so that when the cello enters in the middle it sounds to me terribly pathetic.

You're in a rather unusual position, doing pieces like 'Vesalii Icones' with the Fires and so constantly being confronted by your earlier works. Do you ever get the urge to rewrite?

I often think that I could have done things better, but I'm so preoccupied with the latest thing that I'm writing that there's no question of going back to the old one. And I don't think that the old ones are as interesting as the ones that I'm writing now. I never did. The other day when I did *Vesalii Icones* I thoroughly enjoyed it: I had a lovely time. Even the extravagant gestures that I had crises of conscience about in 1968—I can enjoy them now; the problem is solved.

Do you feel it as a limitation that you've been faced with providing a repertory for the same ensemble since 'Eight Songs' and 'Vesalii Icones'?

No, I don't, any more than a composer would feel the string quartet to be a limitation. It has a much more distinct set of colours than the string quartet, and one can write less abstract music for it. I've not found it an inhibition, and it's been nice to have a group to write for—a great luxury these days.

You've talked about 'Vesalii Icones' in relation to the water-shed of 1969, and another culminatory piece then was 'Worldes Blis'. Your programme note relates that to the music-theatre pieces of the same period, but it wasn't a matter of shared material, was it?

No, not at all. It was a question of working through the experience, in depth, of those pieces. The whole opening section of *Worldes Blis* I wrote in 1966: I don't know how far I got then, but quite a long way into it.

What do you expect of your listeners in hearing the complexity of compositional device in a work like 'Worldes Blis'?

I don't expect much, frankly. A work like that happens on many levels.

I had an experience of this last summer at Dartington, where I did a class on the first movement of the *Eroica Symphony*. I thought that what I was going to say was frightfully obvious, but it turned out that it wasn't: the students had not heard that piece in the way that I had.

What hadn't they heard?

The main point was that there is no exposition, no development and no recapitulation in the foreground, although there is a skeleton of all three things: it goes through the processes. There's a ghost there of exposition, development and recapitulation, but the whole movement is working towards the coda, and the theme is only stated as a continuous line in that coda. The material is slowly assembled and things are tried, rejected, tending towards the theme, so that it's a duplex form. And I think a musical form only really becomes interesting when it's working in two dimensions rather than just one, and preferably in three.

But anyway, if even those students hadn't heard the processes going on in that work, then that makes me realize that no matter how well the public knows and loves a particular piece, they probably don't know how it works.

You don't think in the case of the 'Eroica' you were projecting your own compositional ideas into another work?

Not at all, you can demonstrate it in the notes. On what level Beethoven was conscious of what he was doing I don't know, just as I don't know, when I've finished a piece of my own, on what level I've been conscious of things that I later see have been happening in it. And that the public isn't aware of compositional processes I don't think is at all a thing to worry about, because it really is something that's only of interest to the composer. If you perceive something like that, it's going to be so extremely exciting that you're probably going to want to do something analogous in your own work. And if people want to listen to a piece, want to know it, that's satisfactory enough, because pieces work on so many layers and people's insights and appreciations and participations in the events of a piece are multi-layered too.

But in your own works it's so very clear that processes are going on that the listener is almost bound to want to know what is happening.

Yes, and he's very welcome to find out!

Though there may be difficulties. In the case of 'Worldes Blis', you spent three years on that work whereas a listener is going to spend forty-five minutes with it. There's no recording, so it's not at all easy to gain the necessary acquaintance with the piece.

Yes, I'm afraid that is just how the world works. If we take the *Eroica* again—not that I'm trying to make any comparisons between my own works and it—recordings didn't exist, and the public had very few chances to hear it. Then it did become more often played—but still precious few people have had any insight into it. You only have to listen to the way conductors beat those first two chords with no relation to the rest of the piece.

Still, there are special difficulties with a work like 'Worldes Blis'. It's almost an obverse of the Second Taverner Fantasia, where you start with the ideas and then work them through: in 'Worldes Blis' one gets all the working before one hears the basic idea. So one has either to make a gigantic act of memory or else hear the piece again to find out what the very basis of it was—

Parallel with the Beethoven Third Symphony by the way.

Indeed. 'Worldes Blis' starts, doesn't it, with a duo for harps which is recalled something like half an hour later? Now this is something I find terribly difficult. To begin with, the harp is one of those instruments where one is least aware of pitch: one's sense of pitch would be much more acute if the music were being played by clarinets, say.

Yes, and that's even more of a problem with things like bells and glockenspiels.

So why did you choose two harps for these very involved processes?

I don't know any more. I suspect—this might be after the fact—it was the blandest colour I could find, which would present the material in the most neutral way—rather like a piano, only I couldn't use a piano, obviously.

Why 'obviously'?

Because if you use a piano it sounds like a rehearsal. It's probably a personal prejudice to do with early memories: I remember the Salford Symphony Orchestra when I was a kid doing the Dvořák Ninth Symphony, but the orchestra didn't have enough strings, so the slow movement finished with a D♭ major chord on piano solo.

HOY AND GEORGE MACKAY BROWN

Another important feature of 'Worldes Blis' is the fact that it 'cartographs', as you've said, a landscape you later discovered on Hoy.

Yes, it's the feeling of enormous space, distances, vast perspectives, a sense of solitariness in a large landscape. But obviously I hadn't had the experience of living in that kind of landscape: it was just a hankering after it. If you like, it's an internal landscape, but to me it's got the same feel about it as the pieces that came later, like *Ave Maris Stella*.

When did you first go to Hoy?

1970.

And when did you decide you were going to live there?

Instantly.

And when did you in fact start living there?

The end of 1970, when I stayed for about a month, and it gradually increased after that. In 1973 I got permission to do my house up, and in 1974 I moved in.

Your first Orkney work was 'From Stone to Thorn', which has been followed by many more settings of George Mackay Brown. What appeals to you in his work?

It's probably the internal spring of rhythm, and the images, too: they're not cluttered, and they give the musical imagination scope to explore them without crowding them out.

And so often in George's work there's the cycle of the year expressed on the one hand in the natural seasons and on the other through the Christian legends, and I find both very attractive—the attempt to come to terms with natural phenomena through these terms. That related to his message about the function of art, in *The Blind Fiddler*, I find very attractive indeed.

And quite apart from that, I almost can't read his work without imagining music: it just seems to ask for it.

In 'From Stone to Thorn' and 'The Blind Fiddler' you made a break in using solo voices outside a dramatic context, which you'd tended to avoid before: you have two soloists in the 'Leopardi Fragments', for instance, and the use of solo voices in your choral works is very restricted.

Yes, I think I was a bit scared of doing it, because I don't like the kinds of operatic or oratorio gestures that are associated with solo singing, and I was very anxious to avoid both. But after a good few years of composing I de-inhibited myself.

The other new thing in 'From Stone to Thorn', of course, was the pastoral subject matter, which didn't seem to me at first to relate at all to what you'd been doing before—though when I actually heard the piece I

118

found there was a connection. Did you feel that piece to be a leap into the dark?

I felt it was a leap, but I didn't think it was into the dark. In the mornings I was doing arrangements for *The Boy Friend*, at the rate of one a day, and in the afternoons and evenings I did *From Stone to Thorn*, which just presented itself like that. It took me precisely three days, without premeditation. And I realized then that this was something which was an enormous step forward, and I remember the minute I finished the thing there was a lovely sunset outside, so I went to look at it, and it all seemed to be meaningful in some kind of way.

Was that an extraordinary experience, doing a piece in three days without sketches?

Usually the more lyric pieces you do like that, but with things like the First Symphony, obviously one has to sketch and do a lot of work because a bigger design is more complex to cope with.

THE COMPOSER IN THE COMMUNITY

You've obviously gained a lot from working in Orkney, but do you see yourself as having a responsibility to the people there?

Yes, I do. I suppose I see myself as having a responsibility to try to improve musical standards there, through the festival, through the schools, or in any way that I can. By nature I'm a very quiet and retiring sort of person; I don't like having to deal with a lot of people. But I do enjoy the festival. I make myself do it, and there are great rewards, particularly in writing works like *Solstice of Light* for the St. Magnus Singers or the operas for the schoolchildren. It's very pleasant to see a piece working through people's imaginations, even if it's something that I know a lot of composers would say is totally irrelevant to today's problems—like *Cinderella,* which is a completely escapist fairy story, though I've given it a lot of inflections which make Cinderella's situation relevant indeed. Actually,

119

she relates to those central martyr figures that I've got in the serious operas, though it's done in a very light-hearted way. It's very silly, but it's trying to make some very serious points too—as any funny piece should: it's got to earn its comedy.

And I would like to see a system of apprenticeship, whereby a couple of student composers would come in, say, for three months, helping on *Cinderella* and writing out parts, doing orchestration for me, dealing with the kids, composing other things for them and for all the schools in the country, and working within the community, with the St. Magnus Singers and other groups throughout the islands. It's something I'd very much like to see happening generally. If there were such a scheme here in Camden, for instance, it would be wonderful: composers could go out into the schools and the professional orchestras which exist around this part of London, and you would also have your composers talking about their works, giving lectures and demonstrations, making creative workshops with the kids and with adults if that were feasible, so that they would be teaching not only in the colleges but in the community.

A composer has a very direct responsibility to the community, but his college or university gives him no experience of working in schools or even with symphony orchestras and professional choruses. He's got to find out the hard way and make a lot of mistakes and offend a lot of people unnecessarily. But I can't see that sort of scheme happening because it would need a lot of investment.

It is happening to some extent in Australia, where a lot of money goes into the arts—and it interests me a lot that private money is no good for the arts really, because people always want to invest in something which is going to be prestigious, public and not all all controversial. The exception is Tennant Caledonian putting several thousands of pounds into the production costs of *The Lighthouse* for the Edinburgh Festival, but, for instance, the St. Magnus Festival has no help whatever from the Occidental Oil Company in Orkney, who have quite simply stated that they will not back anything which might give offence to anybody.

You've also begun recently, haven't you, to involve yourself very directly with Orkney issues, as in the cabaret songs for Eleanor Bron.

Yes, they're about the mining of uranium in Orkney, as if it's happening and has happened: they go on into the future. And the music is very funny, and the words are jolly but also very bitter.

Does the same theme underlie 'Black Pentecost'?

Yes, but it's never mentioned. It's just something which is coming in, as in George Mackay Brown's novel, *Greenvoe*, which I took the text from. It could be uranium mining; it could be an oil company; it could be anything. The pollution is there, and the kicking people out of their houses is there, and the destruction of a way of life is there.

The London Symphony Orchestra commissioned it, but when they found out what it was they didn't want to touch it.

SYMPHONIES AND HARMONY

The change in your music since 1970 has, of course, not just been a matter of using Orkney poetry and Orkney subject matter: there have also been deeper changes of style and technique. Could you say something about the magic squares you've been using in 'Ave Maris Stella', the First Symphony and other works?

I suppose, briefly, one is limiting possibilities of transformation very precisely. And in *Ave Maris Stella* it goes further than that, because the nine-by-nine square gives very, very simple results which you can learn and work with—like triads—and very simple rhythmic values too. I've got a crossword-puzzle musical mentality anyway and, as long as I can carry something in my head, I enjoy working with it, and doing that does present little challenges, which I like. Also, I like the associations of those magic squares, and in *Ave Maris Stella* and the symphony, and in *A Mirror of Whitening Light*, I think they give nice results, too.

Previously, I'd been using isorhythmic designs, based on medieval music, and transformation processes where a

121

contour will assume other contours step by step. They relate to the magic square technique, obviously, but that just codifies them very neatly. It does make, too, a kind of thread which works right through the piece, and which I can hear.

And presumably any listener can, too.

Yes, if it's pointed out, and even perhaps if it's not. In *Ave Maris Stella* certainly: there the harmonic movement, from the beginning right through to the end, is very clear. It's the kind of piece where you very quickly know the geography and what stage of the process you're in. And for me it was a pivotal work, where everything became much simpler.

Isn't 'The Blind Fiddler' simpler still?

Yes it is, but the change came in *Ave Maris Stella*, when that direction first became clear, and that was just before *The Blind Fiddler*, which was very much going further in that same direction. And the First Symphony went on in the same direction but then made it more elaborate, quite simply by using more transpositions.

I find that the simpler one's basic concept—a very basic harmonic relationship between three, four, five pitches—the more complex the structure one can develop from it. I don't mean complex on paper: I mean complexity that the ear can actually perceive. And the symphony is, I think, a complex structure in the real meaning of the word. It isn't only a complex surface, but its interior is complex, too.

The harmonic aspect of all these pieces becomes much clearer when the listener becomes aware that he's not got to listen to them in terms of a bass, but that there is often a tenor, as in medieval and some renaissance music, with parts built above and below that, working at specific basic intervals which are referred to again and again. This tenor moves up and down in the orchestra and can be at any pitch level, and once you realize that, it's like opening a door, because if you try to get into the work at the bottom, in the bass, you find the door shut: it won't make any sense, and you'll just have this great wadge of monolithic structure which is incomprehensible. But if you go with your ear to the main part, through the orchestra, and listen in relation to that, you get a great deal more out of it—not only the sense of structure but also the harmonic procedures which take you from point to point in that structure, which make clear the flow of the tenor from instrument to instrument.

It's rather like a lot of early music which was not made to be listened to by an audience: the listener was the person performing a part. Obviously my music is intended to be listened to, but you have to get inside it in the same way, going in and becoming at one point the equivalent of an alto and then a treble and then a bass, so that you are moving around inside the musical space rather than appreciating it from outside.

But it's not always easy to do that. There's no difficulty in the first section of 'Ave Maris Stella', where your tenor is constantly in the cello, but that's not by any means the norm.

No. Well, obviously I don't find it difficult, but I think if you persevere you do hear it, particularly in the First Symphony. If you started listening to the double basses as if they were the actual bass line in the old sense, when all they're doing is making quite surface comment on what's going on in the other parts, it would sound completely strange, like trying to appreciate a painting from a very odd perspective.

But the possibilities of this multi-dimensionality of point of view I find quite fascinating in writing for the orchestra, and I think it is something well worth exploring, trying to take the listener into the sound by quite clear harmonic means, so that he appreciates it in the way that I want him to. Of course, in a piece like my First Symphony, people are always going to be conscious of the ghost of what an orchestral symphony is, and that I like to work with as well: to impose on that my own particular imagining of what an orchestra is.

But there are an awful lot of ghosts.

Yes, yes, tremendous! That doesn't worry me. It becomes a great game in itself—one which I very much enjoy; I rather like the alertness that is demanded. The attitude that people have that they should just sit back and let it all wash over them—I don't like that at all.

Was the harmonic system of the First Symphony and 'Ave Maris Stella' an independent discovery, or did you come to it through analysing other music?

It's not a question of a harmonic system; it's just the way it is, almost. There are some things I would use and others I wouldn't but, if I were asked to systematize it, I'd find it very difficult. After all, composers like Messiaen and Stockhausen and Xenakis make the strangest statements about the techniques which they think they're using when in fact they're doing something else, and I'm a little bit reluctant to go into that kind of discussion, because I might be working at it from one end when what comes out is something completely other, with a logic that I'm not aware of.

I think this happens very often with composers. An obvious example would be Beethoven in his late quartets where, although he thought he was writing diatonic music, it can be demonstrated that in fact he was writing modally with ghosts of keys—in one piece, of course, he actually mentions a mode, so he must have been aware on one level of what he was doing.

As far as the First Symphony is concerned, you talk in your note about tonics and dominants, but they're not a fifth apart. Can you invent these harmonic functions?

Well, modal music did. In plainsong you very often find that you have something functioning as a dominant which is not a fourth or a fifth away. And I don't see why one shouldn't.

But isn't the listener likely to interpret the fifth above your tonic as the dominant?

Oh yes, sure, but then you have a nice interplay.

And how is the listener to know what you are interpreting as the dominant?

He doesn't, but I hope he'll have a pretty good idea by the time the piece finishes. For instance, it works terribly simply in *A Mirror of Whitening Light*, where the dominants are just a fourth up and a fourth down. The basic thematic material works on that interval span, so I just expanded it to cover the whole structure. Whereas in the First Symphony there's much more complex material, and the relationships take what's happening in the small span—in the basic cell—and project that over a large span, so that you get transpositions upon transpositions upon transpositions, branching out from those main notes. I think the only way to trace that is by listening, when I hope the relationships become clear, because on paper, of course, no note looks any more important than another one.

Do you see your earlier works as having tonics and dominants?

One might express it like that, but then I was expressing it to myself more in terms of two pivots, and I hadn't systematized it in a way which would relate to tonal procedure enough to justify calling them tonic and dominant, or substitute dominant, because I hadn't worked out the intervallic contents of coincidences of notes in such a way that it was as much under control as it is in the First Symphony—apart from the obvious things, of a harmony having its preparation and its resolution or, if there is a prepared dissonance, then the dissonance is standing very consciously in lieu of the concord you would expect. It's much more free floating between the pivots, which I thought of as a main pivot and a subsidiary pivot, without the complex hierarchies between them that I've now got. Other notes in the mode that is being used act as subsidiary pivots, and so it's much more controlled in terms of pitch levels and transpositions.

And in the Second Symphony the first movement is much simplified: I've just got two notes which are a semitone apart, and which I've linked to two other notes which are different kinds of thirds away from each other. The main pull is between those two notes a semitone apart, B and B♭, and I've just let the whole of that movement revolve around that, obsessively. While I was working at it, it reminded me particularly of *Tapiola*, and I thought: 'Watch it, mate: you know what happened to this guy after he finished this piece!'

Do you know how the harmony's going to move in the rest of that work?

Yes, I do. I've already got the second movement in my mind and I know it's in F minor.

Not literally in F minor?

No, but it has got a lot to do with F and A♭ in relation to B and D. And I know basically how it's shaped, how it works, so I'm very anxious to get on with it.

Is that always necessary, to start with some feeling of the shape of the thing?

Yes, very much so. I can't work without having a feeling for a work's proportions and the basic material before I put a note on paper. And this particular work is doing formally some things I haven't done before. It stems from a perception which I know isn't a new one, that there are two kinds of wave. In the first the water content of the wave remains static while the form goes through it: for instance, when you look out from my window at the bay, there are wave shapes on it, but if you look at an object, a piece of wood or whatever, it just remains stationary. Then there's the other sort, like you see when you go past the blockship on the way to Hoy on Stevie's ferry, where the tide goes through and the water at the side makes a shape like ringlets, which remains constant while the water is whizzing through: then the form is constant but the content is changing rapidly.

I just started by writing two very different kinds of music, one where the content remains exactly the same and the form is changing, and the other where the form remained absolutely static but the content was changing, and I worked the two against each other. It was just a kind of catalyst that stimulated the original working out of the basic material, and I think I shall follow through the two types throughout the entire piece.

And I'm not the first to have made the observation, because Leonardo drew the two sorts of wave, and also André Gide in his diary for 1897 observed the two kinds on a visit to Normandy. I quite fortuitously came across these two things shortly after I'd started work.

126

Do you know what the tempo relationships of the movements of the Second Symphony are going to be?

The first one's fast; the next one is slow; and the other two are fast and slow, but I'm not quite sure about the order.

Do you see this Second Symphony as relating to the First?

Oh yes, there are lots of things left over from that first one that I'm not pleased with, that are not resolved in that piece.

What kinds of things?

Constructional things. The slow movement: there are some patches in that which I don't think are as tight as they should be—I mean harmonically. Then the transformation of a kind of andante into a scherzo: I'd like to rethink that, not doing the same thing but some other kind of transformation—it's something I'd like to have a second go at. And I think the form of the whole piece is crying out to be developed into something else.

This always seems to be the case, that whenever you finish a piece it's left as the start of something else.

Oh yes, as soon as I put the double bar at the end of a piece, I want to write something else and do that better. Even with the First Symphony, even before I'd heard it in the flesh, I felt, well, here's the beginning of something.

Taking up the second movement of the First Symphony, you've mentioned in your note the example of Sibelius' Fifth, but I don't quite see why you pointed to that as a model. There are lots of examples of slow movements becoming fast ones, even in your own music. What was so special about the Sibelius?

I don't quite know. It was a piece that really caught my imagination, I think partly because he had a lot of trouble with it, so I sympathized with the whole thing. And he literally knocked two movements into one, and that appealed very much.

Do you now see the possibility of several symphonies?

Yes, yes, I do, which just five years ago I would not have seen at all. But I do feel now that having done the Second Taverner Fantasia and *Worldes Blis* and the First Symphony, and some small things like *St. Thomas Wake* and *Stone Litany*, that perhaps it's not too far-fetched to think that possibly I might be able to develop that.

Do you have the feeling that, particularly with regard to your harmonic procedures in these later works, you're part of any grouping among composers?

Not really, no. I suspect that I'm a bit more conscious of it than a lot of people. Some would claim even that it's obsolete to think about harmony, but I don't think it is. Whether you like it or not, when people hear musical sounds happening in relation to each other simultaneously, they're going to project some kind of order on to it, and you might as well help them to project the kind of order that you want to hear, particularly over a long time span. Quite honestly, I think that if we don't think about harmony in that way it's at our own peril as composers. I'm not saying that the kind of organization that I'm doing is going to be any kind of definitive organization, but at least I'm thinking about it, and I know a lot of people aren't.

Of course, although I think it's possible for a piece to establish its own harmonic rules, when somebody comes to hear it, or even when they compose it, it's against the background of other pieces that they've heard, and the rules will operate in relation to other harmonic rules out of other pieces, so they can't be entirely independent. We've not got virgin ears. And certainly no composer, no matter how hard he tries, has got virgin compositional faculties unless he castrates himself, and then nobody's interested in whether they're virgin or not.

You talked earlier about F being central in the second movement of the new symphony, as it is in various earlier works. Do particular focal pitches have particular expressive connotations for you?

Yes—I've not got perfect pitch, by the way: I find it goes up and down according to the weather or something—but yes, very much so. I think a lot of composers have had this. Going back to Beethoven again, he had very definite feelings associated with C minor, or E♭ major, or B major, which he hardly touches, but when he does it's very significant—I'm thinking of the 'Hammerklavier' Sonata and that obsessive B which goes down to B♭ (my own Second Symphony!).

I had a very strange experience recently hearing a recording of *Ave Maris Stella*. I felt terribly uncomfortable, as if the thing had sagged and become totally colourless, as if it was just a wash of pale colour instead of being very sharp and bright. Then I realized what it was: it was all coming out a good semitone down, and instead of being in C♯ the opening was in C.

Are you aware, too, of particular instrumental gestures returning in work after work: things like a glockenspiel going in regular values, or your exaggerated vibrato on string instruments?

No, I hadn't really thought of it in terms of specific instruments, but rather in terms of musical gestures: the same kind of building to a point, making the point, and then moving away. I was very conscious of that in writing the first movement of the Second Symphony, where the most intense moment, towards the end, has got precedents in the first section of the Second Taverner Fantasia and in *Worldes Blis* in the recapitulation of the sonata ghost. And there are other parallels in the thing. At the end it floats off, dissolves, and I realized that I'd done that at the end of the Second Taverner Fantasia and at the end of the second movement of the First Symphony, and inside various other movements.

But I hadn't thought of it in terms of individual instrumental things, and I'm quite interested that you say that.

Well, one thing that goes right through is a sort of trumpet fanfare motif: six or seven notes going upwards, perhaps in an irregular curve, fast. That occurs in the Trumpet Sonata, and 'Prolation' and almost all your orchestral works. I'm not at all saying that you repeat yourself, because obviously the forms and the musical meanings keep on changing, but there is a repertory of instrumental gestures which is quite unusually personal.

Yes, I supppose there is. And thinking of the trumpet gesture which you've just described, yes, I do recognize that, and it does occur in the Second Symphony! And I don't think there's anything I can do about that: it's just there, and it's probably second nature by now.

RESURRECTION

Could you say something about the new opera you're working on, 'Ressurrection'?

That is pretty wild. Everyone will say that, of course, I've gone back to the 1965 extravagant gestures, and it's quite true, but more so and very differently. The knife is much sharper now. And the piece does indeed go back to Act I, Scene IV of *Taverner*: it's really a paraphrase or comment on that.

It sounds as if it's going to be rather more shocking than anything you've done before. And that reminds me of an early article of yours in which you made the point that Beethoven's music was shocking to his contemporaries. Do you see the shockingness of your own work and the shockingness of Beethoven in at all the same terms?

No, because I think Beethoven was a great deal more original than I am. Nobody had ever made a statement anything like those big symphonies.

But there are two aspects to this, aren't there? There's the shockingness of originality and there's the shockingness of the subject matter. And as far as the latter's concerned, you can take the view that art is really always expressing the same things, but in different terms, or you can take the view that it's becoming more uncomfortable because it's going ever deeper into the human psyche.

Music certainly is. I don't think Beethoven would have involved himself in questions which I've touched on in pieces like *Vesalii Icones* and certainly will in *Resurrection*, but then it would have been impossible at that stage to have done so.

130

Those particular regions of insensitivity on the part of the audience, those problems of authority—they hadn't surfaced.

And the possibilities of the vocabulary have been enormously opened up in our own century. I don't think all composers are using them by any means, but they're there.

Part Three

The Composer's Notes on his Works

STEDMAN DOUBLES AND STEDMAN CATERS

While a student at Manchester University, I wrote a thesis for my bachelor's degree on Indian music. Despite its title, borrowed from campanology, the influence of Indian music is very clear in my *Stedman Doubles*, written at that time—1955. The work was originally intended for clarinet and three percussion players, in which form it remained unperformed. When I revised the work in 1968, I compressed the three percussion parts into one virtuoso part and, with Alan Hacker's help, revised the clarinet part in terms of the extended techniques he has developed. The listener familiar with Indian music will recognize something of the slow unfolding of the alap, and the development and extension processes of classical raga performance, as well as the more obvious parallels with tala groupings on the hand-drums. The 'Hindu' influence of Messiaen is also apparent.

The great challenge in composing this, and other works of this period specifically influenced by Indian music (these I destroyed when the Society for the Promotion of New Music rejected them), was the manipulation of the time-scale of music: for I had realized that the rate of the unfolding of events, and the whole concept of form in Indian music, is not of a sequence of closed—or enclosed—events or periods, but that the forms, on both small and large time-scales, are open, defining themselves as they unfold in a way that not only, particularly in slow alaps, concentrates one's attention on each

135

individual pitch and rhythm relationship with maximum intensity and tension, but also bends, or even suspends, perception of the 'passing' of time, so that the formal terms 'too slow' or 'too long', which in western music can be used so often with complete justification, can have no application to such music. _Stedman Doubles_ is a _tour de force_ not only in the obvious technical sense—the extreme difficulty of the writing for instruments, which, in the cadenzas, where the players are 'free', is meant to inspire them to improvise even greater feats of virtuosity—but also a _tour de force_ of sheer concentration for the two performers—as indeed for the listener.

Stedman Caters, for flute doubling piccolo, clarinet, viola, cello, harpsichord and pitched percussion was a revision of an unperformed 1958 work, made in 1968 for the Pierrot Players. This became, however, in the course of its revision, a complete recomposition. It is almost a small concerto for the percussion player, who plays tuned handbells, gongs, marimba, glockenspiel and roto-toms. The formal concept of the work, as well as the treatment of a basic 'set', has much in common with that of _Stedman Doubles_ but, unlike the _Doubles_, it is a gentle work, concentrating on instrumental 'half-light' colours. It has nine sections, with a percussion cadenza between the eighth and the ninth which, in the first performance in May 1968, became, at my instigation, loud and virtuoso. In retrospect, I felt this not to be in the character of the work, and so made it much more reflective and less extrovert. It was also decided to replace the heavy timpani of the first performance with roto-toms, played with the hands. The viola player also plays woodblock, and the viola and cello bow a suspended cymbal.

O MAGNUM MYSTERIUM

O Magnum Mysterium was written in 1960 for Allan Wicks, who was then organist of Manchester Cathedral, and the Choir and members of the Orchestra of Cirencester Grammar School. It was first performed, complete, in Cirencester Parish Church in December of that year.

Writing music for young people presents certain problems—it must be reasonably within their comprehension and technical ability, but there can be no compromise or writing down—children would soon see through such condescension. Also, rehearsal time was far from limitless in the life of a small-town grammar school—the Cirencester choir had 90 minutes each week, out of school hours, and the orchestra a little over two hours, partly in school time and partly out. (Extra rehearsals for particular voices or instruments were difficult to arrange, due to the constant rival claims of other school activities.) Of this time, only a certain proportion could be spent on new music.

O Magnum Mysterium gradually took shape during rehearsals, and the recording differs slightly, even in instrumentation, from the finally published version. A work involving children must not only be 'childproof' but adaptable to the needs and performing abilities of the moment. The inclusion of percussion instruments and some very simple instrumental parts ensured that even beginners could participate.

The whole work is a meditation on the soprano solo heard at the outset—on the wonder and promise of the Nativity. This solo is followed by a carol whose text comes from the Second Shepherd's Play of the Wakefield cycle of mysteries—the shepherds bring the Christ-child gifts—cherries, a bird and a ball 'to go to the tennis'. The first Sonata, 'Puer natus', takes the opening soprano melody and subjects this to displacement and instrumental coloration. Next a second version of the *O Magnum Mysterium* melody, for sopranos, with an additional alto counterpoint; then a carol with choruses in praise of the Virgin Mary, separated by verses tersely foretelling the course of Christ's life and death. The second Sonata, 'Lux fulgebit', has sections where the players, following explicit directions in the score, improvise—a simple and graphic representation of the spread and intensification of the light of the Nativity. The last two carols are, in contrast, calm and reflective—a prayer of the Virgin ('The Fader of Heven') and a final four-part harmonization of the *O Magnum Mysterium* melody.

Although the different sections of this work may be

performed separately, the music heard so far only becomes really comprehensible in relation to the concluding organ fantasia, to which it forms, as it were, a huge 'upbeat'. So far one has heard simple songs of the Nativity and extravert instrumental commentaries, performed by children. Now a virtuoso on music's most complex and developed instrument adds his final comment, in a sequence of variations on the *O Magnum Mysterium* melody, which realizes, on far deeper and more searching levels, the implications of our theme.

SINFONIA

This is the third large-scale work of which the starting-point was the Vespers of 1610 by Claudio Monteverdi. The works in this series, the String Quartet (1961), the *Leopardi Fragments* (1961) and the present Sinfonia, are variations on the Monteverdi original in the sense of Picasso's pictures based on a Goya original, as shown at that time at the Tate Gallery in London. Each work pinpoints, develops and varies some aspect of the original: for instance, the quartet has formal elements from the 'Sonata Sopra Sancta Maria', particularly in its cantus firmus, which bridges sections and is developed organically; the *Leopardi Fragments* apply vocal and instrumental decorative techniques from the solo sections.

The first stage in this compositional process was a thorough study of the Monteverdi. This was effected in part by making a special performing edition of large sections for the choir and orchestra of Cirencester Grammar School, where it was performed by about 250 of our pupils in March 1961. The orchestration involved those instruments available at the school, but included experiments and sketches for the orchestration of the present Sinfonia.

The connection with the original is most clear in the opening movement, stemming from the 'Domine ad adjuvandum'. The strings have an ostinato on four long chords, each chord supporting ever longer and more elaborate melismas on the wind instruments, which function in a solo capacity. A short ritornello for wind alone separates these chords. The movement ends with the four chords, worked cadentially, fortissimo.

The second movement develops the decorative techniques and form of the duo, 'Pulchra es'. The chords of the opening movement are used melodically, and the expressive qualities of these melodies are exploited.

The third movement, like the quartet, is based on the 'Sonata Sopra Sancta Maria', reshaped in the manner of a classical sonata movement. The exposition uses the strings only, except for the second subject, which appears on the horn. The development augments the rhythmic values and intervals of the exposition, the woodwind instruments playing these modified contours against the original shapes which are repeated by the strings. The recapitulation starts with woodwind alone, repeating the modified shapes of the development, the strings and horn entering for the second subject.

The finale is basically slow and uses the form of the hymn 'Ave maris stella'. The phrases of the first section (strings alone) are separated by 'echoes' of one chord each on solo strings. A woodwind ritornello leads to an accelerated, varied version of the first string section, the wind ritornello is then varied, and the work ends with the opening section of the movement, without the string 'echoes' but with two counterpoints added, on bassoon and horn.

The movements follow each other without a break.

SEVEN IN NOMINE

The Seven In Nomine started as a composition exercise for Earl Kim's composition class when I was studying at Princeton University in 1963 and 1964. These I regarded as studies for a large orchestral work commissioned by the London Philharmonic Orchestra, which I had decided to base on John Taverner's In Nomine. In this way I could prepare an experiment with the basic material of the orchestral piece.

139

The first In Nomine was by John Taverner, the sixteenth-century English composer, and was an organ arrangement of the (*Benedictus qui venit*) *In Nomine* section of his mass based on the plainsong *Gloria Tibi Trinitas*. The first piece of the present group sets this In Nomine for string quartet. The second In Nomine is my own, and subjects the plainsong (heard on the flute with octave displacements at the beginning) to a transformation/development process involving complex mensuration-canonic techniques.

The third, again original, is a 'double' of the previous piece, in the sense that the processes are the same, though much condensed. The fourth is an adaptation of a keyboard piece (from the *Fitzwilliam Virginal Book*) by Bull, with the plainsong cantus set for flute with harp, and a dialogue below this, involving imitative techniques pointed by syncopation and cross-phrasing, set for viola and cello.

The fifth In Nomine (original) is one possible realization of a circular canon, with the *In Nomine* plainsong on a cross inside the circle. The notes around the circular stave can be read, from the bottom of the cross, from outside and/or inside the circle, clockwise and/or anticlockwise, in 1 : 1 proportion and/or 2 : 3 proportion, in various clefs. The instrumentation imitates an eighteenth-century chamber organ I have in my studio, which has only four stops, of which the most remarkable is a strident twelfth.

The sixth In Nomine, an instrumentation of a piece by Blitheman in the *Mulliner Book*, a collection of early sixteenth-century organ music, also recalls the sound of this chamber organ, upon which I normally play these pieces. It is characterized by cross-groupings of three times four quavers against four times three quavers.

The final In Nomine is a short recitative, summing up the harmonic implications of Nos. 2, 3 and 5. The work was commissioned by the Melos Ensemble, who gave the first performance of five movements at Wardour Castle Summer School of Music in Wiltshire in September 1965 and the first public performance in London in December of that year.

SECOND FANTASIA ON JOHN TAVERNER'S
IN NOMINE

The Second Fantasia was commissioned by the London Philharmonic Orchestra, who gave the first performance, under John Pritchard, at the Royal Festival Hall, London, on 30 April 1965.

The work grew out of the completed first act of *Taverner*, during the writing of which I had felt that many ideas were capable of a more symphonic development than was possible within the confines of the dramatic context. Some parts of the Fantasia occur in an identical, or almost identical form—for instance, Section 1 forms the orchestral lead into the first confrontation between the King and the Cardinal, who enter on the fanfare; the climactic sixth section accompanies a tableau in Act II where the Jester, as Death, is seen at the centre of a huge Wheel of Fortune, which he revolves, controlling all men's destinies; and Sections 12 and 13 form the orchestral material for the final burning of the Abbot at the stake by Taverner, for his religious convictions.

My main compositional concern was to explore the possibilities of continuous thematic transformation, so that material is in a constant state of flux—the intervallic and rhythmic contours of one of the three main melodic figures are systematically gradually modified until the figure becomes, for instance, its own inversion or one of the other figures. The musical processes involved are perhaps somewhat analogous to the literary techniques employed by Hoffmann in, say, *Meister Floh*, where certain people, spirits and plants are shown to be, within the context of an elaborate 'plot', manifestations of the same character-principle—as is made clear by a line of connection (not a process of development!) that is sometimes semantic.

The work is scored for normal symphony orchestra, including double woodwind, four horns, four trumpets, two trombones and two tubas, and a percussion section including handbells. Formally it comprises thirteen sections. Sections 1 to 6 make roughly a sonata-form movement, with an introduction and coda; Sections 8 to 10 make a scherzo and trio; and Section 12 is a closing extended slow movement.

Section 1: (a) An introduction: the three main melodic figures are heard on solo string quartet in a slow tempo. The first figure is heard on the cello alone (bars 1–5); the second follows immediately on the viola (bar 5); and the third figure follows after a pause on the second violin (bar 15), with the last two notes taken over by the cello. (b) A short development of the introduction, for full orchestra, which gradually becomes faster, culminating in a fanfare for brass, with side drum, which forms an extended 'upbeat' into:

Section 2 (bars 128ff): A quick tempo; two timpani strokes herald a melody in violins I and II in unison, followed by a 'secondary group' whose identities emerge from the violin melody. The section closes with a brief recall of the initial violin melody, with the timpani strokes as before.

Section 3 (bars 219ff): The same fast tempo; this is the development section (if one can speak of a 'development' as such in a work where the basic premise is that the material is always in a state of transformation). The rising figure, starting in low strings with double bassoon and finishing with a reference to the fanfare of Section 1 in high woodwind with harp and side drum, is an introduction to the 'development' itself, and corresponds to the 'short development' of section 1(b). The development proper starts (bar 267) with the chord D—F♯—E—G♯ held on four horns; the constituent intervals in this chord are gradually heard to dominate and unify the whole melodic and harmonic structure of the work. This section explores particularly techniques of isorhythm and mensural canon, and the superposition of elaborate musical structures on a cantus firmus—the long held notes of Taverner's In Nomine are particularly prominent on the oboes at the end of the section (bar 415).

Section 4 (bars 447ff): This is, roughly, a varied 'recapitulation by inversion' of Section 2—starting with the timpani and the violins in unison again. The final cadence of the development—two chords based on the four-horn chord described above, on high woodwind and horns respectively, underlies the opening of the 'recapitulation'.

Section 5 (bars 505ff): A development of the fanfare from Section 1—on high woodwind, horns, trumpets, tubas and side drums. This leads to the climax of the work so far:

Section 6 (bars 539ff): Full orchestra with swirling woodwind flourishes. This is an amplification of the quartet of Section 1(a)—the final bars, with the very prominent drum strokes, crystallize the harmonies of the music so far into three essential chords.

Section 7 (bars 549ff): A slow transition; solo timpani, solo strings (pizzicato) and harp, then two flutes alone, foreshadow the material of:

Section 8 (bars 580ff): A quick tempo. Four varied statements of a ternary group, of which the first and third segments are an ever-developing melody, on a solo woodwind instrument, with melismas branching from it and returning into it with increasing elaboration, accompanied by pizzicato strings.

Between each of the four statements of this ternary group are three interludes on low strings and harp, with double bassoon, of which the most striking feature is the long held notes of the In Nomine cantus, on violin solo, with increasing width of vibrato.

Section 9 (bars 760ff): Solo strings, referring back to Section 1, have' long-held cantus notes, with woodwind figurations in presto, also bells and harp. This section transforms the material in readiness for Section 10, and clinches the harmonic implications of Section 8.

Section 10 (bars 866ff): The form is roughly that of the ternary groups of Section 8, with the interludes omitted, and with transformed material—the first segment is now on violins I, with melismas in increasing profusion on woodwind and pitched percussion and the accompaniment on horns; and in the second segment the double bassoon has the former function of the horn.

Section 11 (bars 1009ff): Transition. The entry of the trumpets, for the first time since Section 6, with bells, recalls the flutes' figure of Section 7, which becomes the bass of the harmony of:

Section 12 (bars 1022ff): The longest section, this is in a slow tempo, and is scored for strings, except for a build-up of chords with brass towards the end.

There are four varied statements of a long melody, combining elements of the three basic figures of Section 1, with increasingly elaborate counterpoints, but always retaining readily identifiable harmony from Section 11.

These four statements are separated by three interludes (as in Section 8). The first interlude, with long-held harmonics and a very slow solo violin melody has an arc-shaped overall contour; the second interlude is much denser, recalling some of the string figuration from Section 3, with an overall contour which curves upwards; the third interlude adds the harp to the ensemble, and the main melody, on violins I, has a jagged outline referring back to Sections 8 and 10.

The third interlude is followed by the fourth statement of the long melody with which the section started, the brass adding the germinal chords of the work in this climactic group.

Section 13 (bars 1202ff): The shortest section, this is scored for woodwind alone, in pianissimo, and refers back to the opening.

ANTECHRIST

Antechrist in some formal respects resembles a concert overture, and stems not only from the fifteenth-century woodcut blocks, 'Traicte de l'Advenement de l'Antechrist' and

'Entchrist', but also musically and more abstractly from my opera, *Taverner*, in which the medieval Antichrist concept, rather than the more literal and familiar figure under that name in 1 John II and 2 John VII, plays a significant part.

The piece starts with a straightforward rendering of the thirteenth-century motet, *Deo Confitemini—Domino*, which is then broken up and superimposed on related plainsong fragments which, both musically and with regard to the related implied texts, turns the sense of the motet inside out. The compositional techniques employed relate more clearly than in any previous work of mine to late medieval techniques, particularly with regard to rhythmic mode and cantus decoration. The listener will readily perceive two extended 'straight' references to the opening motet which interrupt the otherwise continuous transformation processes—in the first of which one line of this is worked into canons by retrogradation and inversion simultaneously, at intervals determined by the harmonic sense, and in the second, at the end of the work, into a double mensural canon.

MISSA SUPER L'HOMME ARME

Missa Super l'Homme Armé started as an exercise—a completion of incomplete sections of an anonymous fifteenth-century mass on the popular song 'L'Homme Armé', in fifteenth-century style. As I was working at this, other possibilities suggested themselves.

In form the work is similar to my *Hymnos* for clarinet and piano—there are three sections, each divided into three subsections, corresponding to the three subsections of the original Agnus Dei of the mass. The eventual treatment stems from the chapter in the *Ulysses* of Joyce corresponding to the Cyclops chapter in Homer. In the Joyce, a conversation in a tavern is interrupted by insertions which seize upon a small, passing idea in the main narrative and amplify this, often out of all proportion, in a style which bears no relationship to the

145

style of the germinal idea which sparked off the insertion. The insertion is often itself a parody—of a newspaper account of a fashionable wedding, or of the Anglican Creed, for instance.

In *L'Homme Armé* the first subsection presents the opening of the fifteenth-century Agnus Dei more or less straight, on the instruments, except that this is prefaced by a harmonization of the tune 'L'Homme Armé' in a popular song style, though not one of the fifteenth century. As the work progresses, however, the incomplete sections of the original Agnus Dei are filled out by music which transforms the basic material into ever more distantly related statements—although the original, with an 'in style' completion, may be present somewhere in the texture, perhaps distorted, setting up unorthodox relationships between foreground and background material.

Two of the 'distortions' are pre-recorded on a 78 r.p.m. disc on which an organ plays first a 'faulty' fifteenth-century completion, in which a sticking needle is simulated in the recording, and later a pseudo-Victorian hymn, with the speaker's words 'Ecce manus tradentis'. Fragments of text from St. Luke intersperse the purely instrumental music throughout.

The work should perhaps be regarded as a progressive splintering of what is extant of the fifteenth-century original, with magnification and distortion of each splinter through many varied stylistic 'mirrors', finishing with a 'dissolution' of it in the last automatic piano section.

PURCELL: FANTASIA AND TWO PAVANS

I have long been fascinated by Purcell's music, but utterly bored by well-meaning 'authentic' performances, which possibly get every double-dotted rhythm right but convey no sense of Purcell's intensity of feeling, sense of fun or sheer outrageousness. I feel the profoundest respect for the 'great' composers of the past, but have no feeling of slavish reverence towards them whatever—after all, they were living, real people, not priests. Already in the early Sixties I *used* Monteverdi's

Vespers in original compositions and, as a preparatory stage in the composition process, reworked several great chunks of that work for the choir and orchestra of Cirencester Grammar School, where I was teaching—and I suspect that, paradoxically, I came a great deal nearer to the sound and spirit of the original, with an orchestration including clarinets and valve-trumpets, than many a 'pure' version, discreetly and beautifully performed. Musical purity in these matters is about as interesting as moral purity. I am sure that many people will consider my Purcell realizations wholly immoral.

In *Missa Super l'Homme Armé* I subjected an incomplete anonymous fifteenth-century Agnus Dei to a sequence of transformations which parodied many styles from different periods including in the score a special 78 r.p.m. recording of an eighteenth-century chamber organ, played on a pre-electric horn gramophone. This same chamber organ, in my cottage in Dorset, with its brazen twelfth stop, determined the character of my realization of the Purcell Fantasia on a Ground, in which the bass clarinet holds the ground bass throughout. This same horn gramophone influenced the realisations of the two pavans, for I have a collection of foxtrot records from the Twenties and Thirties, and my treatment of the Purcell dances was sparked off by these. They are very much preparatory studies for a large orchestral work, *St. Thomas Wake*.

EIGHT SONGS FOR A MAD KING

The flute, clarinet, violin and cello, as well as having their usual accompanimental functions in this work, also represent, on one level, the bullfinches the King was trying to teach to sing. The King has extended 'dialogues' with these players individually—in No. 3 with the flute, in No. 4 the cello, in No. 6 the clarinet and in No. 7 the violin. The percussion player stands for the King's 'keeper'.

Just as the music of the players is always a comment upon and extension of the King's music, so the 'bullfinch' and

147

'keeper' aspects of the players' roles are physical extensions of this musical process—they are projections stemming from the King's words and music, becoming incarnations of facets of the King's own psyche. The sounds made by human beings under extreme duress, physical and mental, will be at least in part familiar. With a soloist of extended vocal range, and a capacity for producing chords with his voice (like the clarinet and flute in this work), these poems present a unique opportunity to categorize and exploit these techniques to explore certain extreme regions of experience, already opened up in my _Revelation and Fall,_ a setting of a German expressionist poem by Trakl.

Until quite recently 'madness' was regarded as something at which to laugh and jeer. The King's historically authentic quotations from the _Messiah_ in the work evoke this sort of mocking response in the instrumental parts—the stylistic switch is unprepared, and arouses an aggressive reaction. I have, however, quoted far more than the _Messiah_—if not the notes at least aspects of the styles of many composers are referred to, from Handel to Birtwistle. In some ways, I regard the work as a collection of musical objects borrowed from many sources, functioning as musical 'stage props', around which the reciter's part weaves, lighting them from extra-ordinary angles, and throwing grotesque and distorted shadows from them, giving the musical 'objects' an unexpected and sometimes sinister significance. For instance, in No. 5, 'The Phantom Queen', an eighteenth-century suite is inter-mittently suggested in the instrumental parts, and in the Courante, at the words 'Starve you, strike you', the flute part hurries ahead in a 7 : 6 rhythmic proportion, the clarinet's rhythms become dotted, and its part displaced by octaves, the effect being schizophrenic. In No. 7, the sense of 'Comfort ye, my people' is turned inside out by the King's reference to sin, and the 'Country Dance' of the title becomes a foxtrot. The written-down shape of the music of No. 3 becomes an _object_ in fact—it forms a cage, of which the vertical bars are the King's line, and the flute (bullfinch) part moves between and inside these vertical parts.

The climax of the work is the end of No. 7, where the King snatches the violin through the bars of the player's cage and breaks it. This is not just the killing of a bullfinch—it is a giving-in to insanity, and a ritual murder by the King of a part of himself, after which, at the beginning of No. 8, he can announce his own death. As well as their own instruments, the players have mechanical bird song devices operated by clockwork, and the percussion player has a collection of birdcall instruments. In No. 6—the only number where a straight parody, rather than a distortion or a transformation, of Handel occurs, he operates a didjeridoo, the simple hollow tubular instrument of the aboriginals of Arnhem Land in Australia, which functions as a downward extension of the timbre of the 'crow'.

The keyboard player moves between piano and harpsichord, sometimes acting as continuo, sometimes becoming a second percussion part, and sometimes adding independently developing musical commentary.

The work was written in February and March of 1969.

WORLDES BLIS

Worldes Blis was composed between 1966 and 1969—a period in which my hitherto consciously integrated and balanced style of composition was shattered by the eruption into musical consciousness of a sequence of violent and dramatic works, whose explosive urgency necessitated a coming-to-terms, through musical means. For instance, the immediate experiences of paranoia in *Eight Songs for a Mad King*, a music-theatre work connected with George III's illness; or the luminous intensities of Trakl's opium-laden poetry in *Revelation and Fall*; or the violent Trinitarian iconoclasm of *Missa Super l'Homme Armé*, a switchback sequence of parodies with the incomplete anonymous fifteenth-century mass as a taking-off point.

Composition of *Worldes Blis* was slow throughout this period—it concerned related musical problems, but on a much larger scale and at a deeper level, and was a conscious attempt to reintegrate the shattered and scattered fragments of my creative persona. I felt this to have been threatened with total extinction by the experience of living through a sequence of works which I could only pen by an act of faith in my own unreasonableness. However, these experiences could not be reasoned out by existence, and *Worldes Blis* seeks to assimilate and build upon them, while maintaining the basic architectural principles employed in my earlier large-scale orchestral music, but exploring unashamedly in length and in depth (to use terms which the medieval composers of the original song might well have understood) the acceptance and integration into my continuing creation of the Antichrist which had confronted me within my own self.

At its performance in 1969 the overall proportions and pacing of *Worldes Blis* gave rise to problems in some quarters. It moves slowly, in long, extremely carefully articulated timespans, with no 'orchestration' as such, but a minimal presentation of the material in such a way as to make the structural bones of the music as clear as possible. After this first performance I withdrew the work, feeling that it was too short, having only explored a fraction of its form-building potentialities. Later, I realized that it was not so much incomplete as germinal, in that its methods lead directly into later large works such as *Hymn to St. Magnus* and *Stone Litany*. Moreover, bearing in mind that ultimately one's music and one's life are inseparably interrelated, I had in its form defined, in a way which made immediate and instinctive sense, the future environment in which I was to compose, when the music, as it were, materialized into a physical landscape. It could well help the listener unfamiliar with its style to relate its architecture to the slowly rolling treeless landscape in which I was to continue the path outlined in the work, with its minimal change as one walks (always totally alone!) among many square miles of hills, but with a constantly modulated meaning according to light, cloud and reflection from the sea. Orkney's wildest island seems to be a natural extension and a living-out of the territory explored and cartographed in *Worldes Blis*.

Throughout the work the material is in a state of constant but very gradual transformation—the melodic, rhythmic and harmonic contours change slightly at each new statement. Although based on the medieval monody, *Worldes Blis*, this melody is only 'discovered' towards the end, played in the percussion section on the bells. The whole work may be heard as a quest for this (pre-existing) material, in one long gesture: from the opening duo for two harps—which is as far removed as possible from the modal monody, while ultimately being proved to be integrally related—through to this appearance on bells. At the same time, the bell tune is deeply embedded in orchestral material derived strictly from it. Although it is present, I felt the 'arrival' or 'resolution' here could not justify any grandiose presentation of the medieval theme, but preferred to state the psychological climate of arrival and resolution through the completion of an architectural arch-form, and by a steadying and crystallization of the harmonic rhythm.

In such a formally complex single-movement work, the kind of programme note which attempts a detailed topography would be self-defeating, but some might find a few selected signposts helpful.

After the aforementioned harp duo, the trombones, then trumpets, have a slowly rising 'cantus' or 'tenor' decorated or 'coloured' by the rest of the orchestra in two long articulations, which are separated by a high cello solo accompanied by stabbing muted trumpets and *divisi* high strings. These two articulations, about twenty minutes in all, form an extended 'upbeat' into a turbulent quick group, where occurs the first real release or 'downbeat' in the work. Its antecedent material is characterized by a widely-spaced rhythmic melody on first and second violins in unison, with high unpitched percussion accompaniment (woodblocks, claves); and the consequent material by heavy brass and deep violent percussion. There follow four development sections. In the first, strictly a 'pre-development', in which material is prepared for subsequent development processes, the harps take up their argument from the opening of the work, this time with

151

melismas from the orchestra. In the second, over one held organ chord, the interest is rhythmic, with high unpitched percussion. In the third, in which a second organ chord is coloured by divisi strings with glissandi, the main argument is divided between three trumpets. In the fourth, the high strings have a quick ostinato, again based on a single chord, with organ melismas and high woodwind figurations. A compressed and more forward-thrusting reworking of the quick antecedent/ consequent leads into a slow conclusive movement in which, as aforementioned, the *Worldes Blis* monody is achieved.

VESALII ICONES

The idea of eventually making a set of fourteen dances based on the drawings of Vesalius came to me when I bought a facsimile edition of the *De Humani Corporis Fabrica* in 1967; the idea of superimposing the Vesalius images on the fourteen Stations of the Cross (slightly modified to include the Resurrection) came much later, and was the direct stimulus to composing the work.

In *St. Thomas Wake—Foxtrot for Orchestra* I had worked with three levels of musical experience—that of the original sixteenth-century 'St. Thomas Wake' pavan, played on the harp, the level of the foxtrots derived from this, played by a foxtrot band, and the level of my 'real' music, also derived from the pavan, played by the symphony orchestra. These three levels interacted on each other—a visual image of the effect would be three glass sheets spaced parallel a small distance apart, with the three musical 'styles' represented on them, so that when one's eye focuses from the front on to one sheet, its perception is modified by the marks on the other glass sheets, to which one's focus will be distracted, and therefore constantly changing.

In the *Vesalii Icones*, such processes are not only present in the music but, more importantly, the dancer has a parallel set of superimpositions—(1) the Vesalius illustrations, (2) the

Stations of the Cross, and (3) his own body. (In the music there are three levels—plainsong, 'popular' music, and my own music derived from the other two—but the three are very much fused and clearly separate identities emerge rarely.)

Each dance starts with the body position of the Vesalius illustration to the sound of the turning of a wheel of small jingles and bells in the band—a ritual significance of bell-signals is present in several of my works. The dancer then moves to express the parallel 'Stations' situation, but the dance is not an attempt to literally act out the Vesalius drawing or the 'Station'—it is an abstract from both, in which the dancer explores the technical possibilities suggested by the Vesalius illustration, in the light of the ritual and emotional experience suggested by the 'Station', in terms of his own body. Similarly, the music is not an attempt to 'illustrate', in a traditional way, the movements or 'moods' of the dancer but works out its own inter-relationships, between my own present 'style' and the fragments of Good Friday plainsong used, my motet, *Ecce Manus Tradentis*, and the work I wrote for the Fires of London at the beginning of 1968, *L'Homme Armé*—each of which is in itself full of musical quotes and cross-references. The dancer himself enunciates in No. 1 the basic rhythmic pattern which generates the rhythmic structure of the work, and in No. 6 the 'Mocking' is effected inside the music entirely—the dancer plays, on an out-of-tune piano, a garbled Victorian hymn (a musical style which I consider almost the ultimate blasphemy)—and subsequently turns this into a cheery foxtrot. The cello soloist sits apart from the instrumental group, near the dancer, and in his eyes, on one level, can become Pilate, Veronica or even a Flagellator, or, on another level, the Anatomy Demonstrator.

In No. 8, 'St. Veronica Wipes His Face', I have developed the idea of the reproduced photographic image on Veronica's cloth in musical terms. The opening music of the movement consists of a line of *Ecce Manus Tradentis* on the cello, accompanied by an inflated plainsong fragment in a musical style which suggests a Victorian daguerrotype. This is imme-diately 'reproduced' in a modified version which suggests to me a hand-operated cylinder phonograph. The raw material from *Ecce Manus* is then bent to resemble a Schenker analysis, but instead of stripping off layers of music to expose ultimately a 'common' skeleton below, the 'skeleton' is heard first and levels are added (the reference to Vesalius is obvious)—but when it would just about become clear to a perceptive ear that the analysis concerned is of the scherzo of the Fifth Symphony of Beethoven, the flute twists the *Ecce Manus* fragment into a resemblance of the scherzo of the Ninth—it is a related but false image. The next 'switch' is to a *L'Homme Armé* mass—not the anonymous fifteenth-century one treated in my own work of that name, but one by Pierre de la Rue. This, with its fairly elaborated canonic structure, is 'X-rayed'—the 'bones' are spelled out as it is played, doubling the notes concerned on another instrument. The 'X-ray' is heard to consist of insignificant common chords and scales—i.e. it becomes absurd. (The percussion player tries to type the rhythm of the treble part as it goes by, but gets it wrong.) The movement ends with a dissolution (fragmentary and garbled reproduction) of the material heard so far—including a reproduction of an incorrectly balanced taping of the opening measures during the performance.

In No. 11, 'The Death of Christ', I kept the piano outside the main argument—the piano mocks, by reducing to absurdity the chords suggested by the counterpoint to the basest currency of added sixths and dominant sevenths. (I became very interested in this sort of musical ambiguity, where, because the music contains disparate, opposed elements, the total effect of these elements can be interpreted by the listener in different ways and on different levels, according to his means.)

In the last dance, 'The Resurrection', the Christ story is modified. It is the Antichrist—the dark 'double' of Christ of medieval legend, indistinguishable from the 'real' Christ—who emerges from the tomb and puts his curse on Christendom to all eternity. Some may consider such an interpretation sacrilegious—but the point I am trying to make is a moral one—it is a matter of distinguishing the false from the real—that one should not be taken in by appearances.

Fides est virtus qua credentur quae non videntur. Nos quidquid illud significat faciamus, et quam sit verum, non laboremus.

SUITE FROM THE DEVILS

The incidental music for Ken Russell's film *The Devils* was written in Orkney in November of 1971. I had retreated to the island with a list of film footages converted into timings, a set of stills from the film to remind me of the contents of each scene, the script, and a metronome and stop-watch. Rather than work on the principle of composing music to coincide with specific points in the action on visual cue—whereby in the recording session, when the conductor sees a certain physical movement on the cue screen he places a certain musical event with it, beating at a given speed so that the next coincidence of physical movement with a given point in the music should be more or less automatic (if it's not he speeds up or slows down a bit!)—I decided to measure the whole thing out in bars of given speeds (suitable for the action), doing the necessary arithmetic to make it as exact as practicable, and composing within that rhythmic framework the sort of isorhythmic structure I enjoy working with in my concert music. With this method, the conductor records the music to the film shown on a cue screen, with a 'click track' in his ear over headphones, which gives the exact speed of the beats of the section—very necessary when accuracy to a fraction of a second is required.

The forces used are small—the basic Fires of London instrumentation (flute, clarinet, violin/viola, cello, keyboards, percussion) plus trumpet and trombone, two more percussion players, and double bass, with, in one number only, two saxophones. Ken Russell and I agreed that it would be as interesting to get as much mileage—change of mood, timbre, etc.—out of a small group, with the aid of varying recording techniques, as to use a full orchestra—and much more economical.

To a film composer, Russell is easy and pleasant to work

155

with—which is as well, since the maker of a film is at a great disadvantage, in that he has no idea how the music will sound or fit until the actual recording session. But Russell and I discussed the music at great length before it was written, together with David Munrow, even to the extent of sending each other up; as when, in the filming of the horrifying and spectacular grand finale of Père Grandier's execution, with hundreds of extras, Russell shouted above the hubbub, 'I think a bit of thick B♭ on trombones there, Max. Must be B♭.' I even got a bit of extra film footage on this scene—musically it would have ended too abruptly, and it required time to cadence properly, so I obtained a few more seconds to allow this, which must be almost unprecedented. One irritation during composition was constant visits by the island postmaster with telegrams to say the censor had cut out several more feet of film, which meant constant rethinking and modification of the isorhythmic schemes.

The sections in the suite are:

1. The fantasia on the Dies Irae—Sister Jeanne's 'obscene' vision of Père Grandier as Christ, walking on the water towards her.
2. The meeting of Sister Jeanne with Père Mignon. This sequence starts with a fight between two women, one a nun, which Russell and I decided would go splendidly to a foxtrot on the plainsong Ave Maria. But when it eventually was seen in context it was too shocking, so the music was ultimately faded in after the fight; the sequence is basically concerned with Sister Jeanne's erotic sentiments towards Père Grandier.
3. The plague.
4. Père Grandier's execution by burning at the stake.

STONE LITANY

Maeshowe, on the mainland of Orkney, is one of Britain's greatest prehistoric monuments—variously described as a temple or a tomb; but according to recent theories it was probably an observatory and sun-temple combined (see particularly Magnus Spence in *The Scottish Review* of 1893). It forms the crux of an extensive system of stone circles, standing stones and mounds up to five thousand years old.

It was broken into by the Vikings, who left runic inscriptions on its walls. Those chosen for this sequence of settings date probably from the twelfth century, and are written in the sixteen-letter script peculiar to Orkney, except for the occasional 'tree-runes', as in the 'Aerlingr' signature in the second setting. There are twenty-four inscriptions, of which I have chosen to set No. 5 (which simply gives the runic alphabet), No. 8, Nos. 19 and 20 and No. 15. (See 'The Runic Inscriptions of Maeshowe' by Bruce Dickins in the *Proceedings of the Orkney Antiquarian Society*, viii (1930).)

I have taken liberties with the settings, assuming that as the texts are in an extinct language (Orkney Norn, a dialect of Old Norse) they will not be readily understood anyway. The voice part can be regarded as a coloured vocalise, forming an obbligato rather than a solo part in its orchestral setting—attempting not so much to set and make sense of the graffiti texts, but to evoke something of the timeless mystery of Maeshowe itself and of the haunted landscape around it.

SYMPHONY NO. 1

When I started my symphony in 1973, I had no idea that that was what it would grow into. The Philharmonia Orchestra had commissioned an orchestral work for 1974, and I wrote a moderately long single movement, provisionally called *Black Pentecost*. The title was taken from the end of a George Mackay Brown poem (which I had set for soprano and guitar, a short

157

time before) concerning the ruined and deserted crofts in an Orkney valley:

> *The poor and the good fires are all quenched.*
> *Now, cold angel, keep the valley*
> *From the bedlam and cinders of a Black Pentecost.*

However, I felt very keenly that this single movement was incomplete, and withdrew it before performance. It was, as it were, budding and putting out shoots, and although I had firmly drawn a final double barline, the music was reaching out across it, suggesting transformations beyond the confines of a single movement.

Its next step was to become two movements in one—the existing movement compressed to become a short slow movement that changes into a kind of 'scherzo' (without the tripartite formal connotations of the name, except as a 'ghost' in the form's far hinterland). This 'lento that becomes a scherzo' is now the second movement.

Next, looking backwards from it, the second movement's first chord sprouted a large new span of music, which eventually became the present first movement. The point of connexion is still aurally present, in that what is now the last chord of the first movement makes, retrospectively, the first chord of the second. The ending of the second movement was no conclusion, so a few months later a slow movement proper followed—and finally, in 1976, the concluding presto.

The scope of the original provisional title had long been outgrown, and I had no other name in mind. Unless one writes orchestral music of a kind that I don't, the climate and economics of the orchestral concert scene are such that one is only very rarely going to hear an orchestral work performed, and even less often adequately prepared. So I have written very few orchestral scores, and have felt much less secure, much less experienced in this field than in chamber music, regarding my few works up to now which involve large forces very much as apprentice scores. Recently I began to feel that I could write the orchestral music, with the orchestral sound, towards which I

158

had been slowly and intermittently working over the years; and, perhaps optimistically, I believed that the present work could mark the possibility of the beginning of an orchestral competence. Hence the title—Symphony.

I had been bolstering my own orchestral composition by analysing various symphonies and large orchestral works in some depth, and in this work I was therefore able to apply various symphonic devices and solutions about which I believe I had for the first time gained some kind of insight. It might be helpful to give the listener some pointers.

The transformation from lento to scherzo in the second movement stems from the first movement of Sibelius's Fifth Symphony, where a moderato sonata-style movement becomes a scherzo. The end of the whole work—the stabbing chords—is an adaptation of Sibelius's solution at the end of this same work of his. The cross-phasing and time-perspective devices in my third movement were developed from the opening of Schumann's Second Symphony, and the overall shape and some of the detailing of formal structure in the last movement came, on the surface level, from 'Don' in Boulez's *Pli Selon Pli*.

The first movement, an allegro, opens with brass chords and pizzicato strings outlining the basic harmonies from which the whole structure stems. The argument proper starts with timpani strokes—F, A♭, G, G, G♭. Although it has a ghost of a sonata form somewhere behind it, there is no first or second subject material as such, and any 'development' consists of transformation processes. These processes are various, and precisely definable according to their position and function in the overall scheme—but as yet there is no common vocabulary to describe such processes, nor to describe the harmonic processes unifying the transformations. However, the transformation processes themselves should ideally make immediate musical sense and be aurally satisfactory, as was the case with the processes of 'sonata form' in Haydn's time. Long before that term was coined and in general use, the message of the music was 'understood' as musical language.

Suffice it to say that there are magic squares involving pitches, note-values and longer time-spans—which not only

159

serve to bring about the gradual transmutations of certain plainsongs into others, but also to form large-scale interlocking isorhythmic cycles. Immediately hearable, I hope, will be the pivotal tonal centre of F, with a 'dominant' of Db—remembering that the musical structure is related to medieval techniques, where a modal 'dominant' is not necessarily a fourth or fifth away from the 'tonic'. Moreover, the voice or part which unifies the harmony is not necessarily a bass line, but often a 'tenor' which usually has long notes, and the harmony is understood upwards or downwards from this. Consequently a (main) chord and its harmonic functions are not those familiar in classical music, though I trust they make sense.

Also very evident is a recurring figure, whose characteristics are one very long note-value, with a crescendo, followed by two very short, loud note-values above and below the pitch of the long one. The exact note-lengths and pitches depend on the music's processes at that point, and are not constant. This figure is first heard on first violins immediately after the timpani strokes mentioned above, and forms a main feature of the movement's arguments until the final crossing multi-voiced statements of it on the woodwind and brass.

The second movement—on D, dominant F#—starts with a statement of the *Ave Maris Stella* plainsong on alto flute (foreshadowed, but not stated plainly, at the very opening of the first movement). This is next split between the three trumpets, and is slowly transformed into the material of a fleeting 'scherzo', whose tempo insinuates itself (in flute, piccolo and clarinet and with solo timpani) across the next alto flute solo, and takes over completely in the following woodwind chords. The movement accelerates towards its eventual evaporation.

The third movement—the slow movement proper (on F#, dominant A#/Bb)—starts with a long tripartite melody on the cellos and becomes another evocation of the extraordinary, almost unearthly, treeless winter land-and-seascape of the Orkney island where I live. But it is not merely descriptive or atmospheric, and the transformation processes to which the melody is subjected are of a different order (paced by a new magic square) more suited to a relaxed motion but, I trust, no less rigorous and musically logical. After a section for strings alone, in which the registration gradually moves upwards, the movement closes with a restructured version of the opening melody on alto flute, and lastly piccolo, which refers back to the alto flute's solo lines in the second movement and prepares the tonality of the last movement.

The finale—presto—has the same tonal outline as the first movement, and is a sequence of long build-ups of tension, often over pendulum-like pairs of chords, the whole being a perpetuum mobile that climaxes in a version of the *Ave Maris Stella* thematic material (the same as at the opening of my work of that name) for unison strings, followed by another for the trumpets. The last stabbing off-beat chords are a fifth above their harmonically 'logical' position. I did not want the last gesture to sound 'final' in a rhetorical way, giving the impression that I thought I had completely worked through and solved the problems posed by the symphony and could therefore afford to write a (falsely) 'affirmative' conclusion. But, the transposition to the fifth, and the off-beat attacks, make audible my impression that the argument was not concluded and that I was aware I had only opened up fields of investigation and not finally harvested their fruits. These final chords put a brake on the generation-transformation processes, no more.

As in my previous works, there is no 'orchestration' as such—the instrumentation functions simply to make the musical argument clear, and one of this size and complexity needs large forces. An unusual feature in the orchestra, however, is the percussion section. It consists of tuned instruments only—the glockenspiel, crotales, marimba and tubular bells, together with celesta, harp and timpani forming together a section of the orchestra which carries as much of the thematic and harmonic argument as any other section—and has material as demanding musically, which is unusual. The orchestral writing is generally very virtuosic, particularly in the brass, and makes great rhythmic demands on the players and conductor.

A constantly recurring feature—not unusual in early music—is the alternation of simple and compound times (say 4/4 and 9/16) while maintaining a regular unit (in this example the semiquaver). In a fast tempo it is all too easy to make the 9/16 into three triplets—which would be fatal, what with simultaneous dependent 'irrational values' and syncopations.

The symphony must play, I believe, for almost an hour and is uncompromising in its demands on performers and listeners. Perhaps it would help to put listeners in a sympathetic frame of mind to the intention, if not the result, to know that possibly the creative artists I admire most are two medieval writers, whose language, to my mind, builds the only sound-structures parallel to the statement made by the medieval cathedrals—Dante and St. Thomas Aquinas. To their vision and example I owe a great deal of what might be positive about my efforts towards a musical logic.

I have dedicated the work to Sir William Glock, as a mark of friendship and of appreciation of his work for contemporary music in his years as Music Controller at the BBC.

THE MARTYRDOM OF ST. MAGNUS

The first task in the composition of the opera was to reduce George Mackay Brown's novel to a workable sequence of scenes suitable for singing, where possible not omitting material but concentrating it. Inevitably, there had to be simplification—Magnus, for instance, is not such a complex character in the opera as in the novel, and certainly not as multi-faceted as in John Mooney's study in depth, published in 1935. The Battle of Menai Strait is reduced to a cypher of a battle—the music itself must fill in the scene set starkly by the two heralds; and the tinkers of the novel are reduced to one. Blind Mary, however, is amplified to become a seer-prophetess figure with, in the first scene, words from another publication of Mackay Brown, and in the last, words based on the poet, at the point where she receives her sight.

The music was composed quickly in the summer of 1976 on Hoy. It is continuous, the scenes being connected by instrumental transitions which either sum up the musical argument of the previous scene or set the mood for the next: often they carry a more developed musical argument than the text settings themselves, where the word-setting determines a clear texture and necessitates a simple dramatic structure. The forces used are small—five singers (one woman and four men who each take several roles), plus flute, clarinet, horn, two trumpets, percussion, harpsichord and celesta, guitar, viola and cello.

The novel has Magnus martyred in a (Nazi) concentration camp; I decided to bring the martyrdom forward to the present, and set it in the place where the opera is performed—an attempt to make audiences aware of the possibilities with us for such a murder of a political or religious figure, whatever his convictions. It is no longer possible to persuade ourselves that 'such things couldn't happen here'. They have in the past and could so easily again if we are not aware of the insidiously persuasive nature of the forces which generate such possibilities.

I have tried to create a musical style that is at once communicative and dramatic, based in the first instance on the Gregorian chant of the Church that Magnus would have known so well, but adapting and extending this to encompass as wide an expressive musical and operatic vocabulary as possible.

A MIRROR OF WHITENING LIGHT

The title 'Speculum Luminis Dealbensis' is alchemical, referring to the purification or 'whitening' process, by which a base metal may be transformed into gold, and, by extension, to the purification of the human soul. It also refers to the Spirit

Mercurius, or Quicksilver, the agent or generator of this transformation process.

Fancifully perhaps, I often see the great cliff-bound bay before my window where the Atlantic and the North Sea meet, as a huge alchemical crucible, rich in speculative connotations, and at all times a miracle of ever-changing reflected light, and it is this which is the physical mirror of the title.

Suitably enough, the 'agent' of the work, in the alchemical sense, is the magic square of Mercurius (in mathematics a square formed of eight-by-eight digits, the sums of whose rows of numbers are the same, read horizontally and perpendicularly). This, suitably used, can generate perfectly recognizable and workable sequences of pitches and rhythmic lengths, easily memorable once the 'key' to the square has been found, by 'courses', in the way that bell-ringers' seemingly arbitrary, and infinitely more complex and long, sequences of permutations are known by heart to experts.

The *Mirror* is scored for single woodwind, horn, trumpet, trombone, one percussion (tuned percussion only), celesta and string quintet, and consists of one compact movement.

The number eight governs the whole structure, and the sharp listener who knows his *Liber Usualis* will recognize emerging from the constant transformation processes at key points eight-note summaries of the plainsongs, *Veni Sancte Spiritus* and *Sederunt Principes*, whose implied texts (if you are prepared to play my game!) have some bearing on the implied alchemy involved.

Over the last few years I have tried to evolve a musical language simple and strong enough to make the complex forms with which I became involved meaningful and audible—particularly with regard to functional harmony operating over and relating large spans of time.

The short opening section attempts to prepare the listener for the different kinds of formal transformation processes and the harmonic areas which the work will explore, fixing in his mind the pitch C from which all the parts spring and to which all return but not by the familiar path of functional tonality. With the solo bassoon statement of a version of *Veni Sancte* the

164

work with its hierarchy of transformations begins slowly to unfold.

The pace quickens and each instrument is given virtuoso solo writing in a sequence of interlocking isorhythmic blocks, the pace becoming eventually allegro and dance-like, just before a climactic re-appearance of the bassoon *Veni Sancte*, which, however, is only deceptively a recapitulation serving as a transition to a slow section refining and crystallizing the harmony of the previous fast music. The work ends with a statement of the key part of the *Sederunt* plainsong on high trumpet.

I have dedicated the work to my former composition teacher at Princeton University, as an eightieth birthday present, Roger Sessions.

SET OF DANCES FROM SALOME

For many years I have longed for the opportunity to write for the ballet, and, even though it meant writing about two hours-worth of music in six months, I welcomed this first chance from Denmark.

Salome was written in 1978 for Flemming Flindt's new company, which he founded upon leaving his position as Artistic Director of the Royal Danish Ballet after fifteen years. *Salome* ran continuously in Copenhagen, six nights a week, for over two months.

In this reading of the bible story it is Herodias who is instrumental in the execution of John the Baptist, while Salome attempts to protect him. Salome herself is portrayed as the over-indulged daughter of rich materialistic parents, who is driven to revolutionary desperation by their power-hunger and crassness.

The work is based on a plainsong for John the Baptist's feast-day, which itself is based on a magic square (it is hard to believe such a thing is coincidental!), and the two elements, plainsong and magic square, generated all of the music, including its formal architecture.

165

Although the work is in every respect 'serious', it had to be 'light' in so far as its first performance and the three-record album were to be by the Danish Radio Light Music Orchestra, under Janos Fürst. The orchestral colours are bright, and the dramatic gestures and formal outlines as clear as I could make them.

For this set of dances I have simply chosen my own favourite bits of the score, bearing in mind that they should build up as logical and dramatic a sequence as is possible under circumstances involving carving up a unified organic whole.

1. The arrest and enslavement of John the Baptist and his followers.

2. High trumpet and tuned percussion fanfares accompany the entrance of King Philip and Herodias, and Herod and Aretas, leading to the murder of Philip and Aretas by Herod and Herodias, and Herod's assumption of power.

3. Salome's duo with the prisoner John the Baptist (harp with strings), at the end of which she sets him free and escapes from the court with him.

4. The River Jordan—John baptizes his followers. Herod enters, unseen by John, who at that point is baptizing Salome. The re-arrest of John.

5. John, imprisoned in a cage, rejects Salome's advances.

6. Herod's banquet—an Arab dance, an acrobats' dance, and a jugglers' dance.

7. Herod attempts to seduce Salome, who rejects him and becomes crazed, dancing naked before the horrified court.

8. The climax of the banquet—John's execution.

9. The 'apotheosis' of John and Salome, who, free of all earthly ties, are united in heaven.

It is probably as well, at a first hearing, to follow the purely musical argument, rather than attempting to grasp, apart from main 'signposts', the 'action' each section of music underlines, while bearing in mind the general style of the balletic presentation—powerful and direct, with plenty of spectacle and pageantry.

THE LIGHTHOUSE

The original inspiration for this work came from reading Craig Mair's book on the Stevenson family of Edinburgh. This family, apart from producing the famous author, Robert Louis, produced several generations of lighthouse and harbour engineers. In December 1900 the lighthouse supply ship *Hesperus* based in Stromness, Orkney, went on its routine tour of duty to the Flannan Isles light in the Outer Hebrides. The lighthouse was empty—all three beds and the table looked as if they had been left in a hurry and the lamp, though out, was in perfect working order, but the men had disappeared into thin air.

There have been many speculations as to how and why the three keepers disappeared. This opera does not offer a solution to the mystery, but indicates what might be possible under the tense circumstances of three men being marooned in a storm-bound lighthouse long after the time they expected to be relieved.

The work consists of a prologue and one act. The prologue presents the court of inquiry in Edinburgh into the disappearance of the keepers. The three protagonists play the parts of the three officers of the lighthouse ship, the action moving between the courtroom, the ship and the lighthouse itself, and the inquiry is conducted by the horn of the orchestra, to whose wordless questions the protagonists answer making the questions retrospectively clear. The court reaches an open verdict. At the end of the prologue the three officers together tell us that the lighthouse is now automatic and the building is abandoned and sealed up, while the lighthouse itself flashes its automatic signal to a rhythm which is reflected in the orchestra.

The main act itself bears the subtitle 'The Cry of the Beast'. The scene is set inside the lighthouse with the three keepers at table in a state of edginess with each other. Arthur is a bible-thumping religious zealot, constantly at loggerheads with Blazes, who has no truck with his hypocrisy; the third keeper, Sandy, tries peace-making moves to keep them apart. When

167

Arthur leaves the table and goes aloft to light the lantern, Sandy and Blazes have a game of crib. They quarrel over this, and when Arthur returns, the atmosphere becomes extremely tense. Sandy suggests that Blazes should sing a cheerful song to help break this tension. This Blazes does, followed by Sandy and Arthur. Each song, though light and superficial on the surface, might be taken as an indication of the inner character and history of the singer. Blazes sings a jolly song about an adolescent's career of crime in city slums leading to murder and the death of his parents. Sandy sings a love song, which, when taken up and accompanied by the other two keepers, takes on a new meaning suggesting that his love life might not have been as innocent as would at first appear. Arthur sings a holy-roller rabble-rousing ditty about God's revenge on the Children of Israel for worshipping the Golden Calf—a projection into God's will and bible history of his own boundless and unexpressed aggression.

Subsequently, the atmosphere turns chill—fog swirls about the lighthouse and Arthur starts the foghorn with the words: 'The cry of the Beast across the sleeping world—one night that cry will be answered from the deep.'

From the mists, ghosts from the past of the three keepers emerge to take their revenge—they might be directly from the songs each keeper sang if these are taken as personal revelations. These ghosts, which we do not see but which the keepers persuade each other are visible, drive them into a state of such guilty desperation that they become crazed. The ghosts call upon Blazes and Sandy to go out with them into the night.

When Arthur comes down from the lightroom, he is convinced that the Beast has called across the sea—the Golden Calf has come to claim his servants. The eyes of the Beast are seen to approach, eventually becoming an all-blinding dazzle. Calling upon God's help, bellowing a hymn, the three keepers move out to defend themselves against this spirit, which they now see as the Antichrist.

At the climax of the storm and the brightest point of the light from the eyes of the Beast, the keepers are replaced by the three officers from the lighthouse ship, played by the same three singers, and the light of the approaching Beast is seen to have been perhaps the light of the lighthouse ship.

From the remarks of the ship's officers, the exact nature of the lighthouse keepers' disappearance is open to interpretation, as is, indeed, whether the officers themselves are trying to persuade themselves that some truth they fear is not so, or perhaps that they are trying to cover something up.

When the relief keepers enter the lighthouse, although they are not seen very clearly, it is more than possible that they are the same three we saw at the opening of the scene, but, as the lighthouse is seen to flash its 'automatic' signal, there is a further possibility that we have been watching a play of ghosts in a lighthouse abandoned and boarded up for eighty years.

The structure is based on the Tower of the Tarot, whose number symbolism is present in the structure of all the music, and which erupts into the surface of the opera in the form of the words sung by Arthur during the card game representing the Voice of the Cards, which on this level transforms the game of crib into a play of fate with Tarot cards, summoning up all the power of their baleful influence.

The work makes extraordinary demands on the singing and acting capacities of the three protagonists, and demands extreme virtuosity from a small band.

CINDERELLA

A few years ago I saw a splendid production of a play of *Cinderella* at St. Mary's Music School, Edinburgh, performed by the children, with incidental music by the young composer on the staff, Geoffrey King. I thought this would make a suitable subject for eventual full operatic treatment for children, with singing throughout instead of speaking.

I had had no experience of writing large-scale music for primary-school children (*The Two Fiddlers*, written for the St. Magnus Festival of 1978, was for Kirkwall Grammar School, and the *Shopping Songs*, written for the primary school in 1979, were very short) and jumped at Glynis Hughes's suggestion of an opera for the primary schools, with help from the grammar school.

This version opens with Cinderella arriving on stage by train, the train being a chorus of small children, carrying engine and carriage cut-outs, and making train noises. Cinderella sings:

'I've to stay with Widow Grumble
Whom I have never seen.
She has three grown-up daughters,
Who are said to be quite mean,
And rude to their au-pair girls,
Most inconsiderate.
I wish I were at home
Watching telly with the cat.'

Despite the train, there only because I still like trains, it becomes clear, particularly in the three Ugly Sisters' songs, that it is Kirkwall where they live with Widow Grumble, with the usual traditional pantomime-style references to and friendly digs at local institutions and dignitaries. The Ugly Sisters are played by older boys in the most outrageous pantomime-dame fashion but without the topical political references and blue jokes which made so much of what the characters said incomprehensible to me as a small child taken to the local pantomime. There are three Ugly Sisters so that, when Cinderella eventually marries the Prince, they are not left to their usual dismal end: Medusa can marry Field Marshal Sir Wellington Bombast Blimp, Hecate can marry Lord Admiral of the Fleet Sir Nelson Drake Victory and Dragonia, Commander-in-Chief of the Royal Air Force Lord Delta Wing Vertical Takeoff—a most meaningful punishment, I thought, for all concerned.

In the Kirkwall Arts Theatre, and on a St. Magnus Festival budget, elaborate transformation scenes were out of the question, so problems like turning a pumpkin into a coach had to be reconsidered, or rather circumnavigated. In this version it is the cat, whom the three Ugly Sisters constantly ill use, who rewards Cinderella's kindness by having her numerous progeny simply bring on the dress, shoes and coach for the Prince's dance, providing the occasion for an elaborate dance number performed by very young children in kitten costumes, in which they eventually escort Cinderella off to the palace, pulling her silver coach.

It is, of course, the Prince's dance in Act II which is the climactic scene. Here the dance styles are designed to show off the choreographic talents on stage, and the music the talents of the pit band. There is first a reel, Orkney-style, for the general company, then a disco-style number for the service chiefs and the Ugly Sisters to clown to, and finally an elegant waltz for the Prince and Cinderella. When midnight strikes, not only does Cinderella leave behind her shoe, with which the Prince identifies her at last, but Ugly Sister Medusa looses her false teeth, Hecate her wig and Dragonia her voluminous bloomers, whereby they are at last identified by their pining military husbands-to-be, who have picked these articles up.

The band is small: a handful of recorders, percussion and strings, with in some numbers a trumpet and throughout an important piano part.

SYMPHONY NO. 2

At the foot of the cliff below my window the Atlantic and the North Sea meet, with all the complex interweaving of currents and wave shapes, and the conflicts of weather, that such an encounter implies.

The new symphony is not only a direct response to the sounds of the ocean's extreme proximity, subtly permeating all of one's existence—from the gentlest of Aeolian harp vibrations as the waves strike the cliffs on the other side of the bay in calm weather, to explosive shudders through the very fabric of the house as huge boulders grind over each other directly below the garden during the most violent westerly gales—but also a more considered response to the architecture of its forms.

I had observed two basic wave-types of potential interest—that where the wave-shape moves through the sea while the water remains (basically) static—as when breakers roll in towards a shoreline (moving form, static content of wave)—and that where the wave-shape is static and constant, while the water moves through it—as when an obstacle, a sea-wreck, for example, protrudes through the surface of a tide race, making a plaited wave-shape behind it (static form, moving content).

While I was first working on the musical potentialities in these two extremely different yet related wave-patterns, and various interactions between them, I came upon André Gide's exact observation of the same phenomenon, noted in an early diary, while on holiday on France's north coast, and also upon Leonardo da Vinci's precise sketches of both wave-types.

These two formulations governed the composition of the new symphony, in small architectural detail and also in long-time spans over whole movements, and more. For example, after the short slow introduction, the first movement proper starts with six 'antecedent' phrases on horns, with 'consequent' phrases on violins, where even the contour is obviously wave-shaped, and the static form and changing melodic and rhythmic content are carefully underlined. In contrast, at the opening of the third movement, the repeating identities of the rhythmic and melodic figures clarify the changing forms of their successive statements.

Deeper in the structure, but I hope still articulate, are large-scale 'pointers', like the surfacing of parallel climactic points of the design in the second and third movements—accelerating strokes on B on the timpani—and, in the fourth movement, the transformation of what starts as a slow movement into a real allegro finale.

It is tempting but, I feel, pressing an analogy too far, to discuss perceptions of wave-motion within wave-motion—the time-cycles of tides and their transforming heights and intensities depending on the moon's cycle—but it is probably useful, in a short note, to discuss the tonality of the symphony, which is the direct musical expression of these perceptions.

Tonality is surely not merely a matter of using a major or minor triad on the music's surface—it is a system of organization, through every aspect of a work, which enunciates it as a coherent whole, governing not only melody and harmony, but rhythm and architecture. The symphony is in B minor. However, the dominant I have used throughout is F, or rather, to be syntactically correct, E♯, exploiting the implied semitonal conflict with the historic, almost instinctive dominant of F♯ which is always in the background of our musical consciousness. The musical space of the tritone B—E♯ is slowly explored throughout the work, being filled in by pivotal steps of a minor third, against the implied cycles of the fifths around B and F minors. This might sound naively simple—but I am convinced that to support a complex structure spanning four substantial movements, an extremely basic unifying hypothesis is necessary, if the ear is to be able to relate surface detail. However, I hope that there is here no easy return to old tonality—I feel there can be no shortcuts to a new musical simplicity by these means, but that tonality might be extended to furnish new methods of cohesion, if it is understood modally, and not necessarily in relation to a bass line, and as of potentially multiple musical significance at any given moment: then it need not reflect a unifying confidence of outlook characteristic of the greatest period of its former exploration, which would be inimical to contemporary experience.

A certain thematic unity is provided throughout by the use of the plainsong *Nativitas Tua, Dei Genetrix*—proper to the birthday of the Virgin Mary, which happens to be my own birthday; this symphony is a birthday gift for the Virgin.

The plainsong is subject to two kinds of transformation process—first, where the intervallic content is gradually and systematically modified to reach an inversion or retrograde (again, a reference to wave-motion), and second, by subjection to permutation by the magic squares of the Sun and of Mars. (These are arrangements of sequences of numbers arranged into squares, so that by reading the square in particular ways, arithmetical constants are given; they are a gift to composers if used very simply as an architectural module, and their astrological overtones are attractive and intriguing.)

The instrumental writing throughout is virtuoso, although

the orchestra used is not particularly large. The percussion section is perhaps unusual, in that it has only tuned instruments—timpani, glockenspiel, crotales, and marimba, which together with the harp, function as a kind of gamelan, and carry as much of the argument as any other division of the orchestra.

The four movements follow the old symphonic plan in outline. In the first, after an introduction containing the germ-cells of all the material for the whole symphony, there is a quick sonata movement, with transformation processes in place of a tonal development, and a systematic exploration of the B—E♯ pivot only throughout, rather than a statement of a tonal centre, followed by a moving away from and a return to that centre.

The second movement is slow, in F minor, with the C♭ (B natural) functioning tonally as the E♯ did in the first. After an introduction, a theme on cellos has virtuoso 'doubles' on bassoon, horn, oboe, and trumpet.

The third movement, with scherzo-and-trio characteristics, has the same tonality as the second, except that the A is natural. Its form consists of super- and juxta-positions of modular 'blocks' of material, the content of which is at first constant, but eventually subject to interior transformation processes, and whose shapes themselves are subject to 'wave-motion', and designed to interlock ever more closely.

The finale starts with passacaglia characteristics, in B minor—a long, slow melody for strings. The pace and the material gradually transform to parallel the first movement and then evolve further into a tonal finale. Towards the end, for the first time in the whole work, the D tonality—hitherto only touched as a step between B and E♯—comes into its own, in preparation for the final cadence on the minor third B and D.

The symphony was composed in 1980. An amusing tailpiece—at the very moment that I wrote the final drumstrokes there was a tremendous, thunderous rock-fall from the cliff at the other side of the bay, opposite my window. I was very shaken, and I hope it is without significance.

GLOSSARY

alap Slow opening section in the performance of an Indian raga.

alto (1) Middle-high register; (2) Singer with a voice in this register, low in the case of women and boys, high in the case of men; (3) Used adjectivally to indicate an instrument of similar range, e.g. alto flute.

antiphon Part of the Christian liturgy, originally a short text said or sung before and after a psalm. In the Middle Ages antiphons were sometimes given elaborate settings and became independent pieces.

antiphony (antiphonal) The practice of having two or more musical ensembles separated in space, usually answering one another.

bass (1) Low register; (2) Singer with a voice in this register; (3) Used adjectivally to indicate an instrument of similar range, e.g. bass clarinet; (4) The bottom part of a musical composition, often directing the harmony.

block-chord Used of a passage of music consisting of chords and very little or no counterpoint.

cadenza Especially brilliant passage, usually for a solo instrument.

canon Kind of composition in which one line is imitated after a short while by one or more others.

cantata Substantial work for voice(s) and instruments.

cantus firmus (cantus) Principal melody in a polyphonic composition; originally applied to medieval and renaissance works but since adopted by composers influenced by music of those periods.

celesta Keyboard instrument producing sounds from hammered metal plates.

chant Alternative name for plainsong, the monodic music of the Church.

chorale Hymn or hymn-like passage in slow block chords.

chromatic Including notes other than those of a diatonic scale.

chromatic scale Scale including all twelve notes in an octave on the piano.

coda Explicitly final section of a movement or composition.

concerto Work for one or more solo instruments and orchestra.

175

concord Chord sounding at rest, usually because it is very clearly in a key.

consonance (consonant) Essentially synonymous with 'concord'.

consort Small grouping of renaissance instruments, such as recorders or viols.

counterpoint Art of making two or more musical lines fit together satisfactorily at the same time.

crotales Small symbols of definite pitch.

development (1) Art of pursuing musical argument, usually on the basis of one or more themes; (2) Section of a movement in which this is prominent.

diatonic Including only the notes of a major or minor scale.

diminished-seventh chord Chord consisting of four pitches separated from one another by a minor third, e.g. C—E♭—G♭—A.

discord Chord sounding ill at ease, usually because it does not belong to any particular key.

dissonance (dissonant) Essentially synonymous with 'discord'.

divisi Body of instruments, using strings or voices, divided into two or more parts.

dominant Pitch acting as a secondary centre to the tonic in a diatonic or modal composition.

dotted-note Note followed in notation by a dot and hence having a duration one-and-a-half times the normal. Double-dotting increases the duration by a further quarter of the original value.

enharmonic Descriptive of a relation between two pitches identical on the piano, e.g. C♯ and D♭.

ensemble Grouping, usually small, of instruments or voices.

exposition The preliminary section of a movement, announcing the basic musical material.

fantasia Used by Davies, with reference to English music of the sixteenth and seventeenth centuries, to denote a musical form proceeding from a single theme.

fifth Interval of seven semitones.

fourth Interval of five semitones.

gamelan Percussion ensemble common in Indonesia

glissando Slide through a range of pitch.

glockenspiel Small xylophone-like instrument with metal vibrators.

harmony (1) The simultaneous sounding of different pitches; (2) The complex of forces existing among pitches.

harmonic (1) Adjective derived from the above in either meaning; (2) Note obtained by causing a string or column of air to vibrate at twice or three times or four times, etc, its normal frequency.

incipit Opening fragment.

In Nomine Composition based on the section beginning 'In Nomine' from the *Gloria Tibi Trinitas* mass of John Taverner.

inharmonic Not belonging to the harmonic series, which is the sequence of natural vibrations of a string or column of air.

interlude Section of a composition separating others.

inversion The turning upside-down of a musical line, with all intervals reversed in direction: e.g. the inversion of C—F—D would be C—G—B♭.

isometre (isometric) Two passages of music are isometric if they are metrically identical, no matter what other differences they may show.

isorhythm (isorhythmic) Two passages of music are isorhythmic if they are rhythmically identical, no matter what other differences they may show.

leitmotiv Musical theme suggestive of a character or emotion, as used especially by Wagner.

marimba Percussion instrument akin to the xylophone.

melisma (melismatic) Ornate decoration to a melody.

mode (modal, modality) Collection of pitches, with to some extent a prescribed hierarchy, forming the normal resources for a piece of music. A piece in the Dorian mode, for example, will use the notes D, E, F, G, A, B and C, with D predominant.

modulation Passing smoothly from one key to another.

monody (monodic) Single line of music.

motif Small musical unit, usually one made clearly important in the surface of a work.

motet Composition with a sacred liturgical text.

music theatre Kind of entertainment marrying music with drama in some unconventional manner (i.e. ballet and opera are not normally considered as music theatre).

obbligato Solo line which is important but not central.

organum Early medieval polyphony, with one or more voices surrounding a plainsong melody.

parody Technique by which the material of one composition, e.g. a motet, is used to create another, e.g. a mass.

pavan Slow dance popular in the sixteenth and seventeenth centuries.

pizzicato Plucking the strings of an instrument, e.g. violin, piano.

plainsong The monodic music of the Church.

polyphony (polyphonic) Music in which one or more lines are sounding at the same time.

positive organ Small organ that can be easily transported.

prolation In medieval notation, division of the semibreve into two or three units.

recapitulation Reprise of musical material, usually towards the end of a movement.

recitative Originally a kind of sung declamation, later applied also to instrumental lines of similar character.

regal Small organ common in renaissance and early baroque times.

retrograde The reversal of a musical line; e.g. the retrograde of C—F—D is D—F—C.

retrograde inversion The simultaneous inversion and reversal of a musical line; e.g. the retrograde inversion of C—F—D is B♭—G—C.

177

ritornello Instrumental refrain.

scherzo and trio Common kind of movement consisting of a vigorous passage followed by a gentler one (the trio) and then by a repeat of the first section.

series (serial, serialism) Arrangement of notes, usually the twelve pitches of the chromatic scale, to make a unit employed constructively in a musical composition.

sonata (1) Composition for (usually) one or two instruments; (2) Kind of movement, also known as sonata-allegro, typical of the first movements of sonatas, symphonies, etc, proceeding most characteristically through sections of exposition, development and recapitulation.

subject Basic musical idea used in a movement, particularly a sonata movement.

tenor (1) Middle-low register; (2) Singer with a voice in this register; (3) Principal line in a polyphonic composition.

texture By analogy with visual sense, the 'feel' of a passage.

theme Basic musical idea.

timbre Instrumental colour.

tonal (tonality) Exhibiting a feeling of key or mode.

tonic Pitch acting as centre in a diatonic or modal composition.

transformation Process of converting one musical idea into another.

transition Passage leading from one section to another.

transposition Changing a melody or other musical unit in register.

treble Highest part of a musical composition.

trio sonata Baroque chamber composition for three instruments and keyboard.

tritone Intervals of six semitones.

variation Change of a musical idea.

virtuoso (virtuosity) Person possessed of high ability in musical performance.

LIST OF WORKS AND RECORDINGS

The following list does not include a substantial quantity of occasional music written for particular concerts or celebrations, but it is otherwise complete. Where appropriate, the name of the author of the text is given immediately after the title, and the name of the publisher after the date of composition. Recordings are indicated by an asterisk*. The first performance is indicated by a cross +. Works without timings have either been withdrawn from performance by the composer or had not yet been performed by the time the book went to press.

Sonata for trumpet and piano, 1955 (Schott)   10 minutes
   * Nonesuch H 71275 (Gerard Schwarz, Ursula Oppens)
   + Elgar Howarth, John Ogdon, Manchester, 1955

Stedman Doubles for clarinet and three percussionists, 1955, revised for clarinet and solo percussionists, 1968   30 minutes
   + Alan Hacker, Tristan Fry, Cardiff University, 23 April 1968

Five pieces for piano, 1955–6 (Schott)   15 minutes
   * HMV ALP 2098, ASD 645 (John Ogdon)
   + Ogdon, Liverpool, December 1956

Alma Redemptoris Mater for flute, oboe, two clarinets, horn and bassoon, 1957 (Schott)   7 minutes
   + John Carewe (conductor), Dartington, 1957

St. Michael, sonata for seventeen wind, 1957 (Schott)   17 minutes
   * Louisville Orchestra LS 756 (Louisville Orchestra/ Jorge Mester)
   + London Symphony Orchestra/PMD, Cheltenham, 13 July 1959

Prolation for orchestra, 1957–8 (Schott)   20 minutes
  + Radio-Televisione Italiana Orchestra/Nino Sanzog,
   Rome, July 1959

Sextet for flute, clarinet, piano, percussion, viola and
cello, 1958, revised as Septet with the addition of guitar,
1972
  + Fires of London, Purcell Room, London, 1972

Stedman Caters for flute, clarinet, harpsichord, percus-
sion, viola and cello, 1958, recomposed 1968   15 minutes
  + Pierrot Players/PMD, Purcell Room, London, 30
   May 1968

Byrd: Three Dances, arranged for school orchestra, 1959
(Schott)   4 minutes

Five Motets for SATB soloists, two SATB choirs and
sixteen players in three groups, 1959, revised with
instruments, 1962 (Boosey)   18 minutes
  + Ambrosian Singers, English Chamber Orchestra/
   Norman Del Mar, London, 1 March 1965

Ricercar and Doubles on 'To Many a Well' for wind quintet,
harpsichord, viola and cello, 1959 (Schott)   12 minutes
  + Dartmouth Festival, USA, 1959

Five Klee Pictures for school orchestra, 1960, revised 1976
(Boosey) $9\frac{1}{2}$ minutes
Five Voluntaries for school orchestra, arrangements of
William Croft (1), Jeremiah Clark (2 and 5), Pierre
Attaignant (3) and Louis Couperin (4), 1960 (Schott)   10 minutes

O Magnum Mysterium, comprising four carols for SATB
choir (no. 4 for SA), two sonatas for fourteen players and
a fantasia for organ, 1960 (Schott)   40 minutes
    * Argo RG 327, ZRG 5327 (Cirencester Grammar
    School Choir and Orchestra, Simon Preston/PMD)
    * Argo 5–BBA 1015 (fantasia only, Simon Preston)
  + Cirencester Grammar School and Orchestra, Alan
   Wicks/PMD, Cirencester Parish Church, 8 December
   1960

Ave Maria—Hail Blessed Flower, carol for SATB choir, 1961
(Novello)   2 minutes
    * Argo RG 446, ZRG 5446 (Elizabethan Singers/Louis
    Halsey)
    * HMV CLP 3588, HQS 1350 (Chichester Cathedral
    Choir/John Birch)

Leopardi Fragments, cantata for soprano, contralto, flute, oboe, clarinet, bassoon, trumpet, trombone, harp and cello, 1961 (Schott) — 16 minutes
    * HMV ALP 2093, ASD 640, Angel 36387, S 36387, Argo ZRG 758 (Mary Thomas, Rosemary Phillips, Melos Ensemble/John Carewe)
    + Dorothy Dorow, Rosemary Phillips, New Music Ensemble/Carewe, London, July 1962

String Quartet, 1961 (Schott) — 13 minutes
    + Amici Quartet, November 1961

Te Lucis Ante Terminum for SATB choir and twelve players, 1961 (Schott) — 11 minutes
    + Cirencester Grammar School Choir and Orchestra/ PMD, Cirencester, 30 November 1961

Four Carols for SATB choir (no. 3 for equal voices), 1961–2 (Schott) — 8 minutes

First Fantasia on an In Nomine of John Taverner for orchestra, 1962 (Schott) — 11 minutes
    + BBC Symphony Orchestra/PMD, Albert Hall, London, 13 September 1962

The Lord's Prayer for SATB choir, 1962 (Schott) — 2 minutes
    + Cirencester Grammar School Choir/PMD, Cheltenham, 1 July 1962

Sinfonia for chamber orchestra, 1962 (Schott) — 20 minutes
    + English Chamber Orchestra/Colin Davis, Festival Hall, London, May 1962

Veni Sancte Spiritus for SAB soloists, SATB choir and orchestra, 1963 (Boosey) — 20 minutes
    + Princeton High School Choir, English Chamber Orchestra/Thomas Hilbish, Cheltenham, 10 July 1964

Five Little Pieces for piano, 1960–64 (Boosey) — 5 minutes
    + PMD, Wardour Castle, August 1964

Seven In Nomine for wind quintet, harp and string quartet, 1963–4 (Boosey) — 14 minutes
    + Melos Ensemble/Lawrence Foster, Commonwealth Institute, London, 3 December 1965

Ave Plena Gracia, carol for SATB choir and organ ad lib, 1964 (OUP) — 2 minutes
    * Argo RG 499, ZRG 5499 (Elizabethan Singers/Louis Halsey)

Ecce Manus Tradentis, motet for SATB soloists, SATB choir, seven wind, handbells and harp, 1964   20 minutes
    + Wardour Castle Summer School Choir, Melos Ensemble/PMD, Wardour Castle, 20 August 1965

Second Fantasia on John Taverner's In Nomine for orchestra, 1964 (Boosey)   39 minutes
    * Argo ZRG 712 (New Philharmonia Orchestra/Sir Charles Groves)
    + London Philharmonic Orchestra/John Pritchard, Festival Hall, London, 30 April 1965

Shakespeare Music for eleven players, 1964 (Boosey)   12 minutes
    + Portia Ensemble/Carewe, 8 December 1964

Shall I Die for Mannis' Sake? carol SA choir and school orchestra, 1965 (Boosey)   3 minutes

The Shepherd's Calender for treble, SATB choir and school orchestra, 1965 (Boosey)   21 minutes
    + Students of Sydney Church Grammar School and Sydney University/PMD, Sydney, 20 May 1965

Notre Dame des Fleurs, mini-opera for soprano, mezzo-soprano, counter-tenor, flute, clarinet, piano, percussion, violin and cello, 1966   6 minutes
    + Vanessa Redgrave, Mary Thomas, Grayston Burgess, Fires of London/PMD, Queen Elizabeth Hall, London, 17 March 1973

Five Carols for SA choir, 1966 (Boosey)   11 minutes

Revelation and Fall (Trakl) for voice and sixteen players, 1966 (Boosey), revised 1980   25 minutes
    * HMV ASD 2427, Angel S 36558 (Mary Thomas, Pierrot Players/PMD)
    + Mary Thomas, Pierrot Players/PMD, Conway Hall, London, 26 February 1968

Antechrist for piccolo, bass clarinet, three percussionists, violin and cello, 1967 (Boosey)   6 minutes
    * Mainstream MS 5001 (Pierrot Players/PMD)
    * L'Oiseau-Lyre DSLO 2 (Fires of London/PMD)
    + Pierrot Players/PMD, Queen Elizabeth Hall, London, 30 May 1967

Hymnos for clarinet and piano, 1967 (Boosey)   12 minutes
    * L'Oiseau-Lyre DSLO 2 (Alan Hacker, Stephen Pruslin)
    + Hacker, Pruslin, Cheltenham, 1967

Taverner (Davies), large-scale opera in two acts, 1962–8 (Boosey) 130 minutes
+ Edward Downes (cond.), Covent Garden, London, 12 July 1972

Purcell: Fantasia on a Ground and Two Pavans, arranged for flute, clarinet, keyboards, percussion, violin, cello and voice ad lib (in Pavan no. 2 only), 1968 (Boosey) 12 minutes
* Unicorn KP 8005 (Fires of London/PMD)
+ Pierrot Players/PMD, BBC Concert Hall, London, 13 January 1969

Missa Super l'Homme Armé (Vulgate), music theatre for speaker or singer with flute, clarinet, keyboards, percussion, violin and cello, 1968, revised 1971 (Boosey) 20 minutes
* L'Oiseau-Lyre (revised version) DSLO 2 (Vanessa Redgrave, Fires of London/PMD)
+ Pierrot Players/PMD, Conway Hall, London, 26 February 1968; (revised version) Murray Martin, Fires of London/PMD, Perugia, 28 September 1971

Worldes Blis, motet for orchestra, 1966–9 (Boosey) 40 minutes
+ BBC Symphony Orchestra/PMD Albert Hall, London, 28 August 1969

Gabrieli: Canzona, arranged for wind quintet and string quintet, Chester, 1969 4 minutes

Eight Songs for a Mad King (Randolph Stow), music theatre for male reciter with flute, clarinet, keyboards, percussion, violin and cello, 1969 (Boosey) 33 minutes
* Unicorn RHS 308, UNS 261, Nonesuch H 71285 (Julius Eastman, Fires of London/PMD)
* Opus One 26 (John D'Armand, University of Massachusetts Group for New Music/Charles Fussell)
+ Roy Hart, Pierrot Players/PMD, Queen Elizabeth Hall, London, 22 April 1969

Eram Quasi Agnus, arranged for seven wind, handbells and harp, 1969 4 minutes
+ English Bach Festival Ensemble/PMD, Queen Elizabeth Hall, London, 19 June 1969

St. Thomas Wake, foxtrot for orchestra on a pavan by John Bull, 1969 (Boosey) 21 minutes
+ Dortmund City Orchestra/PMD, Dortmund, 2 June 1969

Sub Tuam Protectionem for piano, 1969   5½ minutes
   + Stephen Pruslin, Purcell Room, London, 13 January
     1970

Vesalii Icones, music theatre for male dancer and cello with
flute, clarinet, piano, percussion and viola, 1969, (Boosey)   40 minutes
   * Unicorn RHS 307, Nonesuch H 71295 (Jennifer
     Ward Clarke, Fires of London/PMD)
   + William Louther, Jennifer Ward Clarke, Pierrot
     Players/PMD, Queen Elizabeth Hall, London, 9
     December 1969

Solita for flute and musical box ad lib, 1969, revised 1972
(Boosey)   8–12 minutes
   + Judith Pearce, York, 25 June 1969

The Devils, film score, 1970, suite for soprano and eleven
players   25 minutes
   + Mary Thomas, Fires of London/PMD, Queen   (suite)
     Elizabeth Hall, London, 11 December 1971

Points and Dancers from 'Taverner' for ten players, 1970
(Boosey)   18 minutes
   * Argo ZRG 712 (Fires of London/PMD)
   + Fires of London/PMD, Queen Elizabeth Hall, Lon-
     don, 20 February 1971

Buxtehude: *Also hat Gott die Welt geliebet,* arranged for
soprano, flute, keyboards, violin and cello, Chester, 1971   12 minutes
   + Mary Thomas, Pierrot Players/PMD, Dartington, 10
     August 1970

The Boy Friend, film score, 1971, suite for band   25 minutes
   + Fires of London/PMD, Queen Elizabeth Hall, Lon-   (suite)
     don, 11 December 1971

From Stone to Thorn (Brown) for mezzo-soprano, basset
clarinet, guitar, harpsichord and percussion, 1971
(Boosey)   20 minutes
   * L'Oiseau-Lyre DSLO 2 (Mary Thomas, Fires of
     London/PMD)
   + Mary Thomas, Fires of London/PMD, Holywell
     Music Room, Oxford, 30 June 1971

Turris Campanarum Sonantium for percussion solo, 1971
   * L'Oiseau-Lyre DSLO 1 (Stomu Yamash'ta)

184

Ut Re Mi for piano, 1971   3 minutes
  + Stephen Pruslin, Purcell Room, London, 19 January
    1971

Ara Coeli: Lullaby for Ilian Rainbow for guitar, 1972 (Boosey)   5 minutes
  * L'Oiseau-Lyre DSLO 3 (Timothy Walker)
  + Timothy Walker, Queen Elizabeth Hall, London, 18
    September 1972

Blind Man's Buff (Davies, after Büchner), masque for
soprano or treble, mezzo-soprano, mime and dancer with
stage septet and small string orchestra, 1972, alternative
version for soprano, mime and seven players, 1972   20 minutes
  + Josephine Barstow, Mary Thomas, Mark Furneaux,
    BBC Symphony Orchestra/Pierre Boulez, Round-
    house, London, 29 May 1972

Canon in Memoriam I.S. for flute, clarinet, harp and string
quartet, 1972 (Boosey)   variable
  + Vesuvius Ensemble, BBC broadcast, 6 April 1972   length

Fool's Fanfare (Shakespeare) for speaker, two trumpets,
two trombones, ukulele and two percussionists, Chester,
1972   7 minutes
  + Ron Moody, London Sinfonietta/PMD, Southwark
    Cathedral, 23 April 1972

Hymn to St. Magnus for flute, clarinet, keyboards, percus-
sion, viola, cello and mezzo-soprano obbligato, 1972
(Boosey)   37 minutes
  * L'Oiseau-Lyre DSLO 12 (Fires of London, Mary
    Thomas/PMD)
  + Mary Thomas, Fires of London/PMD, Queen
    Elizabeth Hall, London, 13 October 1972

Bach: Prelude and Fugue in C♯ minor, arranged for
flute, clarinet, harpsichord, marimba, viola and cello,
1972 (Boosey)   5 minutes
  * Unicorn KP 8005 (Fires of London)
  + Fires of London, Queen Elizabeth Hall, London, 13
    October 1972

Tenebrae Super Gesualdo for mezzo-soprano, alto flute, bass
clarinet, guitar, keyboards, percussion, viola and cello,
1972   20 minutes
  * Unicorn KP 8002 (Mary Thomas, Timothy Walker,
    Fires of London/PMD)

+ Mary Thomas, Timothy Walker, Fires of London/ PMD, Queen Elizabeth Hall, London, 25 August 1972

Dunstable: *Veni Sancte Spiritus*, arranged with new *Veni Creator Spiritus* for alto flute, clarinet, keyboards, glockenspiel, viola and cello, 1972 (Boosey)   8½ minutes
  * Unicorn KP 8005 (Fires of London/PMD)
  + Fires of London/PMD, Queen Elizabeth Hall, London, 6 May 1972

Dark Angels (Brown) for voice and guitar, 1973 (Boosey)   12 minutes
  * Nonesuch H 71342 (Jan de Gaetani, Oscar Ghiglia)
  + Mary Thomas, Timothy Walker, Dartington, 31 July 1974

Purcell: Fantasia on One Note, arranged for alto flute, basset clarinet, harpsichord, percussion, violin and cello, Chester, 1973   5 minutes
  * Unicorn KP 8005 (Fires of London/PMD)
  + Fires of London/PMD, Albert Hall, 24 July 1973

Renaissance Scottish Dances, arranged for flute, clarinet, guitar, percussion, violin and cello, 1973   10 minutes
  * L'Oiseau-Lyre DSLO 12 (Fires of London/PMD)
  + Fires of London/PMD, Dartington, 29 July 1973

David Peebles and Francy Heagy: *Si Quis Diligit Me*, arranged for alto flute, clarinet, celesta, crotales, viola and cello, 1973 (Boosey)   4 minutes
  * Unicorn KP 8005 (Fires of London/PMD)
  + Fires of London/PMD, Dartington, 29 July 1973

Stone Litany, runes from a house of the dead, for mezzo-soprano and orchestra, 1973 (Boosey)   20 minutes
  + Jan de Gaetani, Scottish National Orchestra/ Alexander Gibson, City Hall, Glasgow, 22 September 1973

Fiddlers at the Wedding (Brown) for voice, alto flute, mandolin, guitar and percussion, 1973–4 (Boosey)   19 minutes
  + Jane Manning, Ensemble Instrumental/Daniel Chabrun, Salle Pleyel, Paris, 3 May 1974

All Sons of Adam, arranged for alto flute, clarinet, celesta, guitar, marimba, viola and cello, 1974 (Boosey)   7 minutes
  * Unicorn KP 8005 (Fires of London/PMD)
  + Fires of London/PMD, Queen Elizabeth Hall, London, 20 February 1974

Miss Donnithorne's Maggot (Randolph Stow), music theatre
for mezzo-soprano with flute, clarinet, piano, percussion, violin and cello, 1974 (Boosey)   32 minutes
  + Mary Thomas, Fires of London/PMD, Adelaide, 9
  March 1974

Bach: Prelude and Fugue in C♯ major, arranged for flute,
clarinet, harpsichord, marimba, viola and cello, 1974
(Boosey)   5 minutes
  * Unicorn KP 8005 (Fires of London/PMD)
  + Fires of London, Queen Elizabeth Hall, London, 27
  November 1974

Psalm 124, arranged for flute, bass clarinet, glockenspiel,
marimba, guitar, violin and cello, 1974 (Boosey)   10 minutes
  * L'Oiseau-Lyre DSLO 12 (Fires of London/PMD)
  + Fires of London/PMD, Dartington, 28 July 1974

John Lennon and Paul McCartney: *Yesterday*, arranged
for guitar, 1974
  * L'Oiseau-Lyre DSLO 3 (Timothy Walker)

Ave Maris Stella for flute, clarinet, piano, marimba, viola
and cello, 1975 (Boosey)   32 minutes
  * Unicorn KP 8002 (Fires of London)
  + Fires of London, Bath, 27 May 1975

The Blind Fiddler (Brown) for soprano, flute, clarinet,
keyboards, guitar, percussion, violin and cello, 1975   43 minutes
  + Mary Thomas, Fires of London/PMD, Freemasons'
  Hall, Edinburgh, 16 February 1976

The Door of the Sun for viola, 1975 (Boosey)   5½ minutes
  + Duncan Druce, University of Surrey, Guildford, 9
  March 1976

The Kestrel Paced Round the Sun for flute, 1975 (Boosey) 4 minutes
  + Judith Pearce, University of Surrey, Guildford, 9
  March 1976

My Lady Lothian's Lilte for mezzo-soprano and six players,
1975   6½ minutes
  + Mary Thomas, Fires of London/PMD, Dartington,
  20 August 1975

The Seven Brightnesses for clarinet, 1975 (Boosey)   3½ minutes
  + Alan Hacker, William and Mary College, Wil-
  liamsburg, Virginia, 12 October 1975

Three Studies for Eleven Percussionists, 1975	5 minutes
Symphony No. 1, 1973–6 (Boosey)	53 minutes

Symphony No. 1, 1973–6 (Boosey)
  * Decca HEAD 21 (Philharmonia Orchestra/Simon Rattle)
  + Philharmonia Orchestra/Rattle, Royal Festival Hall, London, 2 February 1978

Anakreontika for mezzo-soprano, alto flute, harpsichord, percussion and cello, 1976 (Chester)   15 minutes
  + Mary Thomas, Fires of London/PMD, Queen Elizabeth Hall, London, 17 September 1976

Ave Rex Angelorum for SATB choir with or without organ, 1976   3 minutes
  + Pupils of Kirkwall Grammar School/Norman Mitchell, Kirkwall, 18 December 1977

Kinloche his Fantassie, arranged for six players, 1976   5 minutes
  * Unicorn KP 8005 (Fires of London)
  + Fires of London, Dartington, 19 August 1976

The Martyrdom of St. Magnus (Davies, after Brown), chamber opera for five singers and ten players, 1976 (Boosey)   82 minutes
  + PMD (cond.), Cathedral of St. Magnus, Kirkwall, 18 June 1977

Three Organ Voluntaries, 1976 (Chester)   4 minutes
  + Jesper Jørgen Jensen, Vestering Kirke, Denmark, 31 July 1979

A Mirror of Whitening Light for fourteen players, 1976–7 (Boosey)   22 minutes
  + London Sinfonietta/PMD, Queen Elizabeth Hall, London, 23 March 1977

Westerlings (Brown) for SATB choir, 1976–7 (Boosey)   15 minutes
  + Uppsala Academy Chamber Choir, Uppsala University, Uppsala, Sweden, 25 May 1977 (incomplete)
  + BBC Singers/John Alldis, BBC Concert Hall, London, 15 October 1977 (complete)

Norn Pater Noster from *Westerlings*, arranged for SATB choir and organ, 1977 (Boosey)   3 minutes

John Angus: *Our Father Whiche in Heaven Art*, arranged for flute, clarinet, celesta, marimba, violin and cello, 1977 (Boosey)   5 minutes

188

* Unicorn KP 8005 (Fires of London/PMD)
+ Fires of London/PMD, Dartington, 18 August 1977

Runes from a Holy Island for alto flute, clarinet, celesta, percussion, viola and cello, 1977 (Chester)   10 minutes
+ Fires of London/PMD, BBC broadcast, 6 November 1977

Four Lessons for two keyboards, 1978   10 minutes
+ Sylvia Junge, Bernard Roberts, Dartington, 23 August 1978

Le Jongleur de NotreDame (Davies), masque for mime, baritone, flute, clarinet, keyboards, percussion, violin, cello and children's band, 1978 (Chester)   55 minutes
+ Mark Furneaux, Michael Rippon, Fires of London, Stromness Academy Wind Band/PMD, Stromness, 18 June 1978

Salome, ballet score, 1978, suite for orchestra   120 minutes
* EMI 157-39270/2 (score with some cuts, Danish Radio Concert Orchestra/Janos Fürst)
+ Danish Radio Concert Orchestra/Janos Fürst, Circus Building, Copenhagen, 10 November 1978

The Two Fiddlers (Davies, after Brown), children's opera, 1978 (Boosey)   50 minutes
+ Pupils of Kirkwall Grammar School/Norman Mitchell, Kirkwall, 16 June 1978

Dances from 'The Two Fiddlers' for six players, 1978   10 minutes
+ Fires of London, Queen Elizabeth Hall, London, 6 October 1978

Black Pentecost (Brown) for mezzo-soprano, baritone and orchestra, 1979   35 minutes

The Lighthouse (Davies), chamber opera for three singers and twelve players, 1979   75 minutes
+ Richard Dufallo (cond.), Edinburgh, 2 September 1980

Kirkwall Shopping Songs (Davies) for children's choir, piano and percussion, 1979 (Boosey)   20 minutes
+ Pupils of Papdale Primary School/Glenys Hughes, Kirkwall, 16 June 1979

Solstice of Light (Brown) for tenor, SATB choir and organ, 1979 (Boosey)   50 minutes

189

+ Neil Mackie, St. Magnus Singers, Richard Hughes/
Norman Mitchell, Kirkwall, 18 June 1979

Cinderella (Davies), children's opera, 1979–80 (Chester)   50 minutes
+ Pupils of Papdale Primary School and Kirkwall
Grammar School/Glenys Hughes, Kirkwall, 21 June
1980

Little Quartet for young string quartet, 1980   8 minutes

Symphony No. 2, 1980   40 minutes
+ Boston Symphony Orchestra/Seiji Ozawa, Boston,
26 February 1981

A Welcome to Orkney for fourteen players, 1980   7 minutes
+ Pupils of Chetham's School of Music, Kirkwall, 20
June 1980

The Yellow Cake Revue (Davies) for voice and piano, 1980   25 minutes
+ Eleanor Bron, PMD, Kirkwall, 21 June 1980

Yesnaby Ground and *Farewell to Stromness*, piano interludes
from *The Yellow Cake Revue*, 1980 (Boosey)

Piano Sonata, 1980–81   25 minutes
+ Stephen Pruslin, Bath, 23 May 1981

Hill Runes for guitar, 1981
+ Julian Bream, Dartington, 25 July 1981

The Medium (Davies), music theatre for soprano, 1981
+ Mary Thomas, Stromness, 21 June 1981

The Rainbow (Davies), music theatre for children, 1981
+Pupils of Stromness Primary School/Janet Halsall
Kirkwall, 20 June 1981

The Well (Brown), incidental music for a play, 1981
+ Kirkwall, 20 June 1981

Resurrection (Davies), large-scale opera, in progress

BIBLIOGRAPHY

Items marked with an asterisk are reprinted in *Peter Maxwell Davies: Studies from Two Decades*, selected and introduced by Stephen Pruslin (London, Boosey & Hawkes, 1979).

Peter Maxwell Davies: 'The Young British Composer', *The Score* (March 1956), pp. 84–5
———: 'Problems of a British Composer', *The Listener* (9 October 1959), pp. 563–4
Robert Henderson: 'Peter Maxwell Davies', *Musical Times*, cii (1961), pp. 624–7
Peter Maxwell Davies: 'Music Composition by Children', *Music in Education*, ed. Willis Grant (London, 1963), pp. 108–24
John, C. G. Waterhouse: 'Maxwell Davies: Towards an Opera', *Tempo*, no. 69 (1964), pp. 18–25*
Robert Henderson: 'Peter Maxwell Davies's *Shakespeare Music*', *Tempo*, no. 72 (1965), pp. 15–18*
Anthony Payne: 'Peter Maxwell Davies's *'Five Motets*', *Tempo*, no. 72 (1965), pp. 7–11*
Stephen Pruslin: 'Peter Maxwell Davies's *Second Taverner Fantasia*', *Tempo*, no. 73 (1965), pp. 2–11*
Roger Smalley: 'Recent Works by Peter Maxwell Davies', *Tempo*, no. 84 (1968), pp. 2–5
John Andrewes: 'Peter Maxwell Davies's *The Shepherd's Calendar*', *Tempo*, no. 87 (1968–9), pp. 6–9*
Jonathan Harvey: 'Maxwell Davies's *Songs for a Mad King*', *Tempo*, no. 89 (1969), pp. 2–6*
Michael Chanan: 'Dialectics in the Music of Peter Maxwell Davies', *Tempo*, no. 90 (1969), pp. 12–22*
Michael Taylor: 'Maxwell Davies's *Vesalii Icones*', *Tempo*, no. 92 (1970), pp. 22–7*

Peter Maxwell Davies: '*Taverner*: Synopsis and Documentation', *Tempo*, no. 101 (1972), pp. 4–11* (synopsis only reprinted)

Gabriel Josipovici: '*Taverner*: Thoughts on the Libretto', *Tempo*, no. 101 (1972), pp. 12–19*

Stephen Arnold: 'The Music of *Taverner*', *Tempo*, no. 101 (1972), pp. 20–39*

Stephen Pruslin: 'An Anatomy of Betrayal', *Music and Musicians*, xx/11 (1972), pp. 28–30

Joseph Kerman: 'Popish Ditties', *Tempo*, no. 102 (1972), pp. 20–24

Stephen Pruslin: 'Returns and Departures: Recent Maxwell Davies', *Tempo*, no. 113 (1975), pp. 22–8*

Peter Maxwell Davies: 'Pax Orcadiensis', *Tempo*, no. 119 (1976), pp. 20–22

Stephen Pruslin: 'The Triangular Space: Davies's *Ave Maris Stella*', *Tempo*, no. 120 (1977), pp. 16–22*

Peter Maxwell Davies: 'Symphony', *Tempo*, no. 124 (1978), pp. 2–5*

Stephen Pruslin: 'Maxwell Davies's Symphony—an Introduction', *Tempo*, no. 124 (1978), pp. 6–9*

Oliver Knussen: 'Peter Maxwell Davies's *Five Klee Pictures*', *Tempo*, no. 124 (1978), pp. 19–21*

Hans Keller: 'The State of the Symphony: not only Maxwell Davies's *Tempo*, no. 125 (1978), pp. 6–11

David Roberts: Review of scores, *Contact*, no. 19 (1978), pp. 26–9

Eric Hughes and Timothy Day: 'Discographies of British Composers: 2 Peter Maxwell Davies', *Recorded Sound*, no. 77 (1980), pp. 81–93

Judy Arnold, ed.: *Peter Maxwell Davies: the Complete Catalogue of Published Works* (London, 1981)

192

INDEX OF WORKS

GENERAL INDEX

196